FRUSTRATION

REED LAWSON

The Ohio State University

FRUSTRATION

The Development of a Scientific Concept

The Macmillan Company, New York
Collier-Macmillan Limited, London

Library of Congress catalog card number: 65–14073

THE MACMILLAN COMPANY, NEW YORK
COLLIER–MACMILLAN CANADA, LTD., TORONTO, ONTARIO

Printed in the United States of America

SECOND PRINTING, 1966

DESIGN: STANLEY S. DRATE

Foreword

"The Critical Issues in Psychology Series," paperback source books for the undergraduate in psychology, are designed to provide authoritative and provocative reviews of selected topics germane to a spectrum of courses. Each volume offers an original inquiry into major facets of the point at issue and a set of illuminating reports carefully chosen to represent salient positions of historical or current significance. It is expected that this combination will afford instructor and student opportunity to read stimulating, even challenging, argument with primary sources in hand.

Few topics are as fundamental to behavior dynamics as that of frustration. This volume provides a sound experimental treatment of this concept and relates it as well to the problems of personality dynamics. A feature of *Frustration* is its use of the concept as an example of a scientific construct and of the way in which it has developed. The author has given us a unique case history, which should prove of unusual value to the many instructors who wish to give their students a first-hand look at the manner in which behavioral scientists attempt to solve their semantic problems.

Reed Lawson has spent several years in active experimentation on this problem, and he is coauthor of a comprehensive review of the experimental and theoretical literature. After receiving his doctorate in experimental psychology from the University of Missouri in 1955, he moved to The Ohio State University, where he is presently associate professor of Psychology.

MELVIN H. MARX, *General Editor*

v

Preface

THIS BOOK IS FIRST A SURVEY OF THE INTRIGUING RESEARCH and theorizing that have been concerned with the particular psychological topic "frustration." Its emphasis is on experimental and experimentally oriented work, but this is not meant in the narrower sense of "experimental" as a specific subdivision of the field of psychology. Experimental research on frustration from areas such as personality, child, and social psychology is also included.

Second, and I think equally important, this volume is meant to illustrate by a specific example the ways in which psychologists go about translating a term that originated in the nonscientific vernacular into a technical scientific term.

When a scientific discipline first begins to emerge, its developers begin by looking at the world in the same way an intelligent layman does. But the layman's vocabulary for describing his world contains many terms that are too imprecise, ambiguous, or complex for effective scientific discourse. One of the earlier phases of the development of a science, therefore, involves the evaluation and reinterpretation of this vernacular description of its subject matter.

All branches of science seem to go through this phase of vocabulary readjustment. The history of the older disciplines suggests that many of the vernacular terms eventually disappear, or they are radically altered in meaning. Nevertheless, the transition from the prescientific to a scientific language is an interesting and important phase in the history of any science.

Although psychology has now blossomed into a relatively mature science, with all of the accompanying technical language (and jargon), there are many psychologists still willing to try to define their research problems in terms familiar to the "intelligent layman." This practice has been a mixed blessing for the development of a scientific psychology. The use of familiar terms is perhaps beneficial in that it shows how an increasingly technical field maintains some contact with reality as perceived by the layman. But it is also a hindrance, for the prescientific language of psychology is a jumble. Select a word from the natural language pertaining to psychological phenomena, and it may be a mixture of (a) a description of behavior, (b) a description of a variable preceding behavior, and (c) a hypothesis about the causes of behavior. Clearly, attempting to incorporate such terms into a rigorous scientific language invites difficulties because of disagreement in the acceptance of the sense of such words or phrases.

Over the years scientific psychology has pretty well rid itself of lay terms freighted with mystical or supernatural connotations, because they were clearly unworkable. But other prescientific terms remain appealing, and they vex, and tantalize because they seem to refer to real variables, to real behavioral phenomena, or to useful hypotheses, simultaneously or separately. Of the many such terms that concern psychologists today "frustration" is one. In the course of reviewing work on frustration, we will indicate how this particular research area reveals the process of developing a scientifically useful concept out of a prescientific idea.

REED LAWSON

Contents

PART TWO: The Selected Readings

FRUSTRATION

PART ONE

Inquiry and Argument

CHAPTER I

An Overview

WHEN WE SAY THAT A PERSON IS "FRUSTRATED," WHAT do we mean? It could simply be a description of observed behavior, used in the same manner as when we describe a person as "walking," or "talking." But describing someone as being frustrated is rarely used in that simple way. The use of the term is more akin to saying that a person is "anxious," or "motivated." We *seem* to be talking about behavior, but we are actually implying much more. We are implying that a person is behaving in a certain way *because* certain things have happened to him. We are not just describing behavior, we are also suggesting causes of that behavior. To put this more technically, we are stating, or at least inferring, certain relationships between independent and dependent variables.

Now the problem becomes one of accomplishing two things: (1) identifying the *relevant* independent and dependent variables from all those available, and (2) trying to discern characteristics common to the classes of variables—independent and dependent separately—that will enable us to give these classes generic names if possible. The typical approach to this double-headed problem involves two procedures: developing theoretical concepts and developing empirical concepts. Let us consider these two in turn.

Theoretical Strategies

The redefinition of a term is primarily a linguistic process. Defining terms in science, and stating how these terms are to be used in conjunction with one another, can loosely be called theorizing. Because it is my contention that the primary problem with respect to the concept of frustration has been that of clarifying this term in a scientifically useful manner, it should be no surprise to find that there has been a relatively large amount of theorizing about the word. This theorizing has taken several forms which when considered in a rough chronological manner nicely illustrates, at least in part, how a vernacular term is metamorphosed into a technical term:

1. Frustration is accepted at face value as a unique, independent topic for study. At this stage there is an attempt to construct a "theory of frustration" that is relatively self-sufficient. The term may be, and usually is, discussed against a background of what we know about behavior in general. The integration of the term into this total context is of secondary importance.

2. Next, there is an attempt to discuss the phenomena presumably covered by the term in the language of some broader behavior theory. This procedure preserves the integrity of the term itself in that it still accepts the term as identifying a usefully distinct subject matter.

3. Finally, there may be the essential absorption of the term into some other, presumably more "basic," formulation. The term is no longer, for scientific purposes, considered to be a necessary topical entity. It is not always easy to say when a term has reached this stage, because the theorists involved may themselves never use the term. However, a valid case can be argued with respect to at least one contemporary theory that has in fact absorbed the concept of frustration into a larger context, and this will be shown in Chapter II.

The three-stage theoretical process will be used to organize the theoretical writings on frustration in the next chapter. Hindsight being clearer than foresight, the reader should not get the impression that the development of theorizing is necessarily as orderly as depicted herein. In the particular case of frustration theories there *is* a rough chronological correspondence to the phases outlined. But this is not always the case. Nor does this apparently smooth transition do justice to the complex interrelationship between empirical research of various kinds and the development of frustration theory. The process with respect to frustration theory has, however, been remarkably orderly and serves as an excellent example of what has happened in a more haphazard fashion to many terms in psychology.

Research Strategies

Ultimately, whatever theory of frustration is developed, the term must be related to manipulations and/or observations of a sort that can be reliably reproduced in a laboratory. It should be obvious that a research report would be unacceptable if it merely said "We frustrated S for the first nine trials" and left it at that. Any reader's immediate reaction would be "Yes, but what was *actually done* to S?" No matter what kind of theoretical definition of frustration is developed, this definition in turn must finally be traced back to a set of directly observable events.

Let us call this the development of an empirical, or operational, definition of frustration, which may take any of several courses. An investigator may leap directly from the vernacular to an experimental analog and thence to a theoretical reformulation of the term. Or the process may be vernacular, then theory, then experiment (then, possibly, revise theory). Some investigators may work only in contact with the vernacular and the experimental, leaving their theory only implicit (if, indeed, they actually have any at all).

In any case, all of these approaches share in common the important role of translating either the vernacular term, the theoretical derivative, or both, into the language of experimental operations. This is a very crucial step, although psychologists disagree among themselves as to the proper order of the theoretical and empirical steps. This disagreement is clearly reflected in the research literature on frustration.

When the step toward empirical definition is taken, it may also be of several forms (or strategies). Unlike what was suggested with regard to theorizing, there is no essential or even apparent chronological order to the kinds of empirical definition that may occur. The forms are these:

1. Take an arbitrary "frustration" procedure, and examine the response consequences of this procedure. In any experiment, of course, nearly everyone does this. What is referred to here is the case in which an investigator repeatedly relies on the same basic "frustration" procedure over a number of experiments as he explores the relevance of different variables. Whenever an experimenter follows this basic strategy while at the same time discussing

his results in terms of the general concept of frustration, he is implying that there is a "thing" we can call frustration—that is, results gained with one frustrating procedure can be generalized to other frustration procedures. Clearly there is at least an implicit theory as to the nature of frustration involved in such a practice.

2. Take an hypothesized behavioral outcome of frustration, and see the many ways in which this can be produced. This, for any one investigator, still implies some (perhaps unexpressed) concept of the kinds of independent variables that are frustrating.

3. State the essential characteristic of a frustrating situation, the effects of this upon behavior, and then try a variety of experimental situations to see if this relationship holds. This is not a practice carried out by any one experimenter, actually. Rather, it represents the sum of the efforts of types 1 and 2 above by many different investigators. The third chapter of this volume will attempt to perform the third function verbally (as opposed to experimentally) while organizing the empirical frustration data around the first two strategies.

FRUSTRATION AS A STATE OF THE ORGANISM

Along with its concern with vernacular terms, early academic psychology inherited a concern with "inner processes." Later, behaviorism, which has had a profound but not total influence on American psychology, argued that the proper subject matter of psychology was the behavior of "the other one" (Meyer, 1921). Therefore, inner states of the organism—being inaccessible to direct observation—could not be the focus of attention in a truly scientific psychology. This point of view has never been thoroughly accepted by all psychologists. Especially when trying to deal with prescientific concepts, there is still a strong inclination to appeal to inner states. Such a tendency is quite clear when we look at a concept like frustration. The layman's definition of frustration is not simply a definition in terms of dependent and independent variables. There is a very strong implication that when an organism is frustrated some very important things are happening *inside* the organism, especially in terms of the organism's *feelings*.

The only organism whose inner, private experience we ever "observe" is ourself. With respect to any other organism the status of their inner feelings is always an inference—an inference, so the behaviorist argument goes, based on our observations of overt behavior and our knowledge of external events preceding that behavior.

It can even be argued that this same inferential process is intimately related to our "observations" of our own private experience. Skinner has developed this argument quite brilliantly (1957, 1963). His point is that when we "observe" our own private experience, we are primarily *talking* about such inner events. But how do we learn to talk about them? On the basis of the language-training practices of those around us. So, in fact, we are still relying upon others' perceptions of our overt behavior and its observable antecedents as the basis for learning to talk about our own inner experience.

In short, the concern with frustration (or the effects of frustration) as an inner state of the organism inevitably turns out, from the behavioristic viewpoint, to be a psuedo problem. Ultimately the real problem is always one of identifying the observable antecedents and behavioral consequents and formulating generalizations about the relationships of these events.

Here is a specific example of a problem that is faced in turning a prescientific concept into a scientific one. Different psychologists have somewhat different views on just how serious a problem this is, and how to solve it, but it presents a good case history.

FRUSTRATION AS A HYPOTHETICAL CONSTRUCT

Closely related to the conceptualization of frustration as an inner state of the organism is the view of frustration as a hypothetical construct. A hypothetical construct, in general, posits some mediating event occurring between specific antecedent and consequent conditions that causes these conditions to be related. This mediating event is "hypothetical" because the exact means of measuring, or otherwise operationally identifying, the mediating process is unspecified.

Any number of terms in psychology have been used in this way at one time or another. It might be suggested, for instance, that "drive" is some sort of unspecified arousal factor that mediates the relationship between the operation of food deprivation and the observation of heightened responsiveness after this operation. In this case, *drive* is being defined in such a way as to make it a hypothetical construct.

Although the use of hypothetical constructs is not currently enjoying great popularity in experimental psychology, many influential psychologists have in the past argued for the utility of this practice (for example, Tolman, 1949; Krech, 1949). Their argument is that such constructs are logically necessary to explain how the observed antecedent and consequent conditions are, in fact, related to each other. By including hypothetical content in the definition of the term, it is further reasoned, future researchers are oriented toward the experimental specification of these mediators. This, in fact, has definitely happened. In the case above of the illustrative example of drive, much research has been directed toward the search for "arousal mechanisms" in the brain (compare Bindra, 1959). It seems almost inevitable, unless we return to metaphysics, that such mediating events (if they exist) must turn out to be physiological in nature.

There are many psychologists who feel that, for the present at least, adequate psychological theory can be developed solely in terms of psychological variables. To name just one, Skinner (for example, 1950) has repeatedly argued against the premise that psychology must go outside its own data in order to find order in these data. Without getting into the controversy about physiological bases of behavior, Marx (1963) has also urged that psychological terms should first be defined exclusively in terms of the kinds of measurements and manipulations that psychologists can make. When psychological constructs are defined solely in terms of relationships between operationally definable events, these constructs are called intervening variables. Intervening variables, it is claimed by many, are satisfactory definitions of psychological terms both for theory construction and communication of empirical findings.

Marx (1963) went on to suggest a form of evolution for psychological terms composed of three essential steps: (1) prescientific definitions, (2) definitions in the form of hypothetical constructs, and (3) definitions in the form of intervening variables. The fundamental dimension of this evolution is that of an increasing operational specificity of terms, or a decreasing surplus meaning to terms.

My analysis of the changes in the term *frustration* closely parallels the evolution suggested by Marx. I have chosen the formulation of the process described above under "Theoretical Strategies" (and elucidated in Chapter II) partly to avoid immersing the reader too deeply in the problems of the philosophy of science, but there is another reason, too. Although increasing operational clarity is one of the most important ways in which psychological terms must change if they are to be useful, this is not the only way in which terms can (perhaps should) change. Some of these other dimensions of change are indicated throughout Chapter II.

FRUSTRATION AS A CLINICAL PROBLEM

A special "real-life" source of ideas about the role of frustration in behavior is applied clinical psychology. Nearly all definitions of neurotic behavior include some references to chronic frustration as a symptom of neurosis, and many theories of neurotic behavior regard past frustrations of certain kinds as part of the cause of neurosis. Psychotherapy can be regarded in part as aimed at helping people to recognize past or present sources of frustration and to learn to deal with them.

Although some of these clinically derived theories are quite interesting, they too tend to be laden with prescientific conceptions of frustration and its effects. Understand that this does not mean they are wrong, only that they need clarification. Clinical data has quite specifically influenced some of the theories and experiments we are about to consider. Although we will not deal with clinical literature per se, the reader should remember that this has been a rich source of hypotheses about frustration. Presumably a clarification of frustration as a scientific concept should ultimately lead also to a more effective technology regarding its pathological effects.

CHAPTER II

Theories of Frustration

"SELF-CONTAINED" THEORIES

Psychology has always had its popularizers, and some academic psychologists have always been willing to talk in scholarly tones about matters that were little more than common-sense notions. On the other hand, much of the "pure" research that was conducted during psychology's early years was so "pure" as to seem to have little connection with the real world of human behavior.

Beginning in the 1930's, however, a new trend began to take definite shape in the discipline. As psychologists developed a more sure hand with scientific technique, and developed more uniquely "psychological" research methods, a renewed ambition to apply these methods to more complex problems emerged. Oversimplifying the situation somewhat, one might say that during the 1930's intercourse between the psychological ivory tower and the real world increased rapidly.

One of the complex, real-life problems to which attention turned was that of frustration. The especial impetus for the interest in this particular topic was undoubtedly the work of Sigmund Freud. Just as it was altering Western thought in general, Freudian theory was gaining a measure of respectability in academic psychology. But psychologists quickly found that an appreciation of Freudian principles was one thing; to use them as a basis for experimental research was quite another (Sears, 1943, 1944; Hilgard, 1952). So psychologists adopted the strategy of developing their own theories to cover some of the same ground as Freud had done in a somewhat too metaphorical and mentalistic way.

Of course, not all psychologists interested in frustration were heavily influenced by Freudian hypotheses. After all, as I repeatedly emphasized in the first chapter, the concept existed in the natural language anyway.

For various reasons, then, during the late 1930's and the 1940's a number of independent theories of frustration began to appear. These theories all shared several things in common: They identified "frustration" as a somewhat unique topic in its own right; they tended to define the term by a rather simple set of operations, and they concentrated on hypothesizing about the behavioral effects of this phenomenon. Four major theories of this sort developed: Rosenzweig's "heuristic" theory, the frustration-aggression theory, the frustration-regression theory, and Maier's fixation theory.

Rosensweig's Frustration Theory

In 1934 Saul Rosenzweig, then a research assistant in the Harvard Psychological Clinic, published a "heuristic" classification of types of reactions to frustration (Rosenzweig, 1934). A heuristic device is one that is intended to stimulate research (as opposed to being the more or less "final word" on a subject). Practically all psychological theories are heuristic in that sense, of course. What Rosenzweig specifically meant was that he intended his classification to become the basis of a measurement device in the personality assessment field and then, in turn, a basis for experimental research.

A more complete formulation of Rosenzweig's theory appeared in 1938 and is reprinted in the Readings section of this book [1].[1] An essentially similar version of the theory appeared in 1944. Briefly, because the details are given in Rosenzweig's own words in the Readings, the theory consisted of three major points. First, there was a very global definition of frustration conceived of as the occurrence of an obstacle that prevented the satisfaction of a need. The reader should note that the term *need* covered much more in the 1930's than it usually does today—it was being used as more or less equivalent with the broad concept of motivation. Second, and

[1] Bracketed numbers refer to readings in Part Two.

perhaps the best-known feature of this approach, was a classification of types of reactions to frustration. Although Rosenzweig, in an attempt to be comprehensive, had a very elaborate classification scheme of frustration reactions, the concepts that have caught on most in psychological writing are his concepts of Extrapunitive, Intropunitive, and Impunitive reactions. These are still regarded by some people as forming a potentially useful dimension of personality, and it is undoubtedly the aspect of the theory that has received the most research attention. Finally, Rosenzweig addressed himself to the concept of frustration tolerance. He made two assertions that, in a general way, are subscribed to by many psychologists: (1) frustration tolerance tends to increase with age, and (2) there is some sort of "optimum" amount of frustration that an individual should experience at a particular developmental level in order to attain maximal frustration tolerance. A somewhat unique aspect of his 1944 presentation was an attempt to place frustration on the same dimension with physical disease and stress.

Rosenzweig's theory clearly exemplifies those characteristics of early frustration theories mentioned previously. It treats frustration as a rather unitary concept; true, Rosenzweig hedges on this a bit—as when he says that frustration tolerance may not be uniform across all areas of experience—but the general tone of all of his writings is to use the term *frustration,* unqualified, as the subject of his hypothesis sentences. The primary emphasis is on reactions to frustration. There is a definite connection with psychoanalytic thought.

It is not the intent of this chapter to get into empirical frustration research too deeply, but a few words about the sorts of empirical activity closely related to the various theories is clearly in order.

There have been two main lines of work stemming, at least in part, from Rosenzweig's ideas. One of these concerns memory and preference for success and failure experiences as a function of age (Rosenzweig, 1933, 1943, 1945; Rosenzweig and Mason, 1934). This was regarded by Rosenzweig as an indication of frustration tolerance—recall of, or a tendency to resume, tasks on which the subject had previously failed was regarded as showing higher frustration tolerance. These researches formed the basis for Rosenzweig's statement that frustration tolerance generally increased with age. Actually, as we shall see later, this whole problem of subsequent reactions to differential success and failure on a series of tasks is a very complicated area, with many variables entering into the reactions obtained.

The second line of research concerns Rosenzweig's classification of reactions to frustration. After some initial attempts with relatively simple response categories, Rosenzweig eventually developed a projective test designed to evaluate people's reactions to frustration primarily along the extrapunitive (and so on) dimension (Rosenzweig, 1945). This test consisted of a series of cartoon pictures depicting potentially frustrating situations of a wide variety. The subject's task was to describe the verbal reaction of the person shown as being frustrated in each picture. These verbal responses are then classified by the tester according to Rosensweig's scheme of frustration reactions. This test is generally known as The Rosenzweig P-F (for Picture-Frustration) Test. Most of the research using this instrument has not been concerned with the direct manipulation of specific independent variables. This is not really surprising, because the theory itself does not deal with this problem to any great extent. Instead, the test has been used primarily as a measure of an aspect of personality, and research with it has been mainly of the correlational sort in which standing on the P-F test is related to other personality characteristics measured or inferred from the subject's status on other personality tests or things such as social class.

By many psychologists' standards, then, Rosenzweig's theory would seem to have failed to generate the experimental work he urged in his early writings. Research on a theory, however, tends to go in the directions indicated by the theorist. Rosenzweig's primary interest was in rather broad aspects of personality. Very little of a specific nature was ever said by him about the mechanisms of, for example, the development of frustration tolerance. Accordingly, his theory never provided the primary impetus for the study of the details of such mechanisms.

This early frustration theory also never generated the kind of controversy that characterized some of the theories we are about to cover. The reason seems simple: it is, after all, primarily an outline of a number of possibilities. No very specific hypotheses are ever offered, no independent variables are really clearly pinpointed, the dependent variables are rather global concepts, and no relationships between independent and dependent variables are very definitely stated. In short, there is very little to argue about. You might choose to use his classification scheme, or you might not, but there is very little to question.

The Frustration-Aggression Hypothesis

The second major frustration theory developed during this period came from a group of social scientists working at Yale's Institute of Human Relations. This theory was presented in a book entitled *Frustration and Aggression*.[2] It represented an attempt to translate into formal terms ideas that were to be found in the early writings of Freud. It is also quite clear that its authors felt that common-sense observation supported the formulation too.

The basis of this theory consisted of two seemingly very straightforward propositions: (1) the occurrence of frustration always increased the tendency for an organism to respond aggressively, and (2) whenever an organism responded aggressively this was prima-facie evidence of the previous occurrence of frustration. *Frustration* was defined as interference with a behavior sequence normally leading to a "goal-response"—or reinforcement of the type specified in the various versions of the Law of Effect. Aggression was behavior that was reinforced by the occurrence of injury to an organism (or some substitute for an organism). In brief, frustration ultimately leads to aggression; aggression always implies that frustration has occurred at some previous time.

Dollard *et al.* meant this only as a starting point for dealing with the apparent realities of frustration and aggression in nature. The paper by Miller [2] in the Readings section attempts to clarify this point. From the initial assumption about the relationship of aggression to frustration, they proceeded to discuss four main classes of factors that determined the specific form that aggression might take as a result of frustration.

First of all, they discussed the conditions that could affect the *strength* of the tendency to respond aggressively to frustration: (1) The greater the strength of the goal-response sequence interfered with, the greater would be the tendency toward aggression. All of the examples of this principle that were given in the book concerned manipulating response strength by manipulating what are sometimes called "drive" conditions, but presumably stimulus and reinforcement variables could also be at work. (2) The greater the amount

[2] John Dollard *et al.*, *Frustration and Aggression* (New Haven: Yale University Press, 1939).

of interference with the goal-response, the greater would be the tendency toward aggression. The details of how to define *amount of interference*, were, unfortunately, spelled out primarily by anecdote rather than formally. (3) The more frustrated response sequences occurring over a period of time, the greater would be the tendency toward aggression. This is analogous to the effect of the summation of weak stimuli in psychophysics, and intuitively it has some appeal. As Dollard *et al.* readily admitted, however, the span of time involved during which the effects of several frustrations can summate is obviously important, but there was no empirical evidence as to what this span might be. In effect, the authors were saying that the tendency toward aggression is a function of the severity of the frustration. Severity of frustration is determined either by the strength of the response interfered with, or by the degree of interference itself, or by the summated effect of several frustrations.

The second set of conditions which Dollard *et al.* discussed reflected their realization that the environment (organismic and inanimate both) does not take aggression passively. The tendency of an organism to respond aggressively is frequently punished, both in the case of specific outbursts and in principle. Punishment tends to inhibit the expression of aggression. Therefore, the degree to which aggression will be expressed—at least overtly—is a function of the amount of punishment expected for a particular aggressive act. Combining this principle with those discussed in the preceding paragraph, Dollard *et al.* made the assumption that the positive and negative tendencies toward aggression summated algebraically to determine whether aggression would occur overtly after frustration.

Having sketched in at least a broad outline the factors that determine whether aggression occurs overtly at all, these theorists then turned to a third set of conditions affecting the frustration-aggression relationship: those factors determining whether aggression would be direct or indirect. They began with the hypothesis that the strongest aggressive tendency is directed toward the agent perceived as being the source of frustration; less direct forms of aggression were less strongly aroused by frustration. But following the considerations of the two preceding paragraphs, the most direct form of aggression may be the most strongly inhibited. When this is the case, then indirect forms of aggression will occur. In general, this is called *displacement of aggression* (a term invented by Freud, incidentally). Its most common anecdotal illustration is the case of the man who, refused a raise by his boss, is hostile (aggressive) with his wife. Displacement, however, is generally thought of as referring only to a change in the *object* of aggression. Dollard *et al.*, therefore, extended the reasoning of this paragraph to cover the case in which the *form* of aggression as well as the object was changed. Such changes are due to the interaction of positive and negative tendencies with respect to the most direct form of aggression, and to the fact that there is a hierarchy of indirect forms of aggression that increase in likelihood of occurrence as stronger (more direct) forms are inhibited.

Finally, the formal development of the theory concluded with a discussion of the implications of the fact that the successful occurrence of aggression is itself reinforcing. This leads to a decreased tendency toward aggression for the time being, just as successful eating temporarily reduces the tendency to eat. In psychoanalytic terms this is called *catharsis*. Combining the principles of displacement and catharsis lead to a final conclusion: there is an inverse relationship between the tendency of different forms of aggression to occur. As one form is inhibited, others are strengthened; when one form occurs, others are weakened. This rather clever deduction enabled these theorists to assert that they had proved what they had started out by assuming: that there is a "functional unity" to the various behaviors to which the term *aggression* can be applied.

An examination of *Frustration and Aggression* would reveal, far more than space permits here, the extent to which this theory was rooted in a common-sense approach to frustration. In that book there is an extremely heavy reliance on anecdotal illustration. What Dollard and his four coauthors did, primarily, was to dress up both vernacular and Freudian notions about frustration in a more behavioristic language, and to try to develop an internally consistent use of this language in the formulation of principles and hypotheses. This was no small step forward, but it was only a step in the right direction. Of course, that is all the authors claimed it to be.

The lasting contributions of this theory, aside from the evolutionary one that I have chosen to emphasize, are hard to evaluate, for two reasons. First of all, just because the theory was so closely tied to Freudian and thence to everyday concepts of how frustration worked, it was not always easy to evaluate which of these three sources contributed most to subsequent research and thinking on frustration in general or even frustration-aggression in particular.

Secondly, we have already noted that the theorist himself usually takes the lead in indicating the lines along which the theory and its attendant research should develop. Because of World War II, such guidance never really developed in the case of this theory. All of its contributors became involved in the war effort, and when they returned to civilian pursuits a few years later they were generally interested in other problems. So frustration-aggression theory of a behaviorist sort lost the impetus that its creators might normally have given it.

There are some important exceptions to the last statement. During the war years Professor Clark L. Hull, also of Yale, published the first complete version of his enormously influential stimulus-response-reinforcement behavior theory (Hull, 1943b). After the war N. E. Miller (one of Dollard's co-workers) returned to one aspect of the frustration-aggression theory, displacement, long enough to formulate it in the sophisticated S-R terminology that Hull was making popular (Miller, 1948). Basically, Miller showed empirically that rats taught to aggress against other rats would generalize this response to another stimulus (a baby doll), but only if the original stimulus for aggression (the other rat) were absent. He related this to Hull's concept of stimulus generalization, and it is generally regarded as a very skillful integration of different theoretical points of view. With reference to the original frustration-aggression theory from which his thinking apparently stemmed, however, there is a very significant feature of his experimental demonstration. "Aggression" was induced in his subjects by specific reinforcement type of learning, not by frustration (unless *frustration* is defined very broadly). Electric shock was turned on when two rats were in the experimental cage together. When, in the process of leaping about, one struck the other in a fighting manner, shock was turned off. As would be expected, the rats learned to strike one another, but what bearing has this on the assumption that the occurrence of aggression always implies the previous occurrence of frustration? Presumably (see Miller [2]) this was supposed to be an iron-clad principle.

Probably the most persistent user of the assumptions of the original frustration-aggression theory has been R. R. Sears (another of its five original authors). Sears's primary interest has been in the field of child behavior and development. Both his interpretations of aggressive child behavior under controlled observational conditions (for example, Sears, 1950) and in the home environment (for example, Sears, Maccoby, and Levin, 1957) contain thinking with the mark of the frustration-aggression theory still clearly discernible.

Perhaps one lasting contribution of this theory was in the sphere of social psychology (for example, Berkowitz, 1962). The analysis, or at least suggestion, by Dollard *et al.* of how such frustrative factors as economic depression and repressive forms of government can lead one group to aggress against another seem to have continued to be supported as a reasonable theory. Of course, as Dollard *et al.* themselves often pointed out, many other social scientists were thinking along these same lines at about the same time, so it is not an entirely unique contribution of this theory alone. But that is one of the troubles with a theory that is so closely rooted to common-sense notions—it is hard to isolate the ideas that might not have arisen had not the theory been stated just as it was. In fact, there may be no such ideas.

As for research, frustration-aggression theory either stimulated or was compatible with a great deal of it. A recent extensive review of this theory (Yates, 1962) cites over 50 empirical studies relevant to it, and that is probably a conservative indication of related research. This research extends right up to the present time, too. So we might say that the theory is in the curious position of having no really staunch advocates, yet certainly not being "dead," either. This is not really so unusual, though. The essential vagueness of its quasi vernacular terms, and the looseness of its broad, although formalized, principles make it an easy touchstone for a variety of empirical studies.

Except for its rather sweeping opening assumption, *Frustration and Aggression* was a carefully written exposition of the theory. Not as much can be said for all of its criticisms, especially many that came soon after its publication. One of the early difficulties stemmed from a too literal interpretation of the opening assertion that frustration always produced aggression. As you followed the remainder of the description of the theory above, it should have been clear that this statement was never intended to mean that frustration was always immediately followed by *direct, overt* hostility. Yet this was a charge brought against it repeatedly until finally the members of the Institute had to explain themselves all over again in open court, so to speak (for example, Miller [2]; Sears, 1941).

Yates (1962) has detailed the various criticisms brought against this viewpoint in later years. They seem to reduce to three general kinds of objections: (1) Is there really a unitary aspect of behavior we can call "aggression"? (2) Are all frustration situations essentially alike? (3) Couldn't aggression occur for other reasons—as through learning that it is reinforcing in its own right (not in reducing frustration) in certain situations? Objections of type 1 and 2, of course, are not surprising when we consider the origin of the terms themselves. Objection 3 simply is an outgrowth of the vagueness of terms implied in the two preceding criticisms. As noted earlier, Miller (1948) seemed to support this criticism in practice. As I have implied before, these are not really criticisms unique to the work of Dollard *et al.* These kinds of difficulties are inherent in the early development of a scientifically useful term with a dubious lineage.

The Frustration-Regression Hypothesis

In his extensive writings, Freud had many things to say about frustration, because it was a central concept in his system. Not all of the hypotheses he expounded fitted neatly together into an integrated whole. In addition to the frustration-aggression hypothesis, Freud also suggested the notion that frustration could cause an individual to revert to modes of action that had characterized his behavior at an earlier developmental stage. This is called the frustration-regression hypothesis.

This hypothesis was formulated in more objective terms capable of experimental test by Barker, Dembo, and Lewin [3]. Their theoretical formulation and its experimental support were largely confined to this single monograph. (It is the summary of the monograph that appears in the Readings section of this book.)

Just as in the case of the work of Dollard *et al.*, Barker, Dembo, and Lewin [3] reformulated the Freudian notion into the conceptual scheme called field theory, for which Kurt Lewin was the prime spokesman. Although field theory has not been without its influence on psychology, its terminological details never became an important part of the psychological vocabulary, so no attempt will be made here to discuss the hypothesis in Lewin's own terms.

Basically, the frustration-regression hypothesis requires that we begin with a developmental picture of how certain kinds of behavior change with maturation. Then subjects are exposed to a frustrating situation, and an assessment of the developmental stage of their subsequent behavior is made. If the behavior is that which is characteristic of an earlier developmental stage than the subject showed just prior to frustration, regression is said to have occurred. The situation chosen by Barker, Dembo, and Lewin [3] for the investigation of this phenomenon was a play situation, with children of different ages serving as subjects.

First the children's "constructiveness" of play was rated with respect to a standard set of toys. A developmental scale of constructiveness was generated from these ratings. Then the children were given an opportunity to play with a much more interesting set of toys in the same experimental room. Finally, they were arbitrarily removed from these toys and given the opportunity of playing with the standardization toys again. During this period the more desirable toys were still visible behind a wire barrier. It was found, as indicated in the article in the Readings, that constructiveness of play with the standard toys decreased following frustration, suggesting regression (that is, a return to an earlier developmental level of behavior).

The Barker, Dembo, and Lewin [3] concept of a frustrating situation is quite similar to those already discussed. A barrier is interposed between the subject and a very desirable goal; in other words, a goal-response is interfered with. This theory is also similar to the preceding ones in that it argues that there is a characteristic kind of reaction to frustration—in this case, regression.

Just as with the other theories, however, there is some hedging with respect to the inevitability of this reaction and also with respect to the inclusiveness of this response category. This weakness is revealed in their discussion of children being exposed to "strong" or "weak" frustration. Objectively, all Ss were exposed to the same situation. Whether frustration was strong or weak was judged by the experimenters *on the basis of reactions of the children to other aspects of the situation besides the toys.* That is, the intensity of frustration for a given child was estimated from his behavior with respect to the barrier and toward the experimenter, primarily. Now, are these also to be judged on a "regressive" scale? Logically, they cannot, because then a statement about the relationship of intensity of frustration (defined by behavior toward the barrier) and amount of regression (defined by behavior toward the toys) would boil down to a statement that more regression is correlated with more regression. This statement might be true, but this experiment could not prove it, because then the investigators would be using their dependent variable to *define* the characteristics of their independent variable. In other words, they would be proving their hypothesis by accepting their hypothesis a priori. Now, Barker and his colleagues were too smart to make such a simple mistake, so what they ended up doing was admitting the possibility that behavior other than regression also occurred as a result of frustration. This was exactly the problem faced by Dollard *et al.* But the rationale of how this other behavior related to regression, and the extent to which non-regressive behavior could be predominant over regressive behavior was not spelled out in such detail as Dollard *et al.* gave to the same questions with respect to aggressive behavior.

So we are left with a "theory" which we don't know how seriously to take. Ignoring, for the moment, the main methodological criticisms of the Barker, Dembo, and Lewin [3] research, it is not clear whether regression is just one of many possible reactions to frustration, or whether it is conceived to be the most prominent feature of most reactions to frustration.

Freud, at least in some of his writings, seemed to feel that regression was a major and very important effect of frustration. Of course, his "regression" is not exactly the same as the more limited operational definition put forth by Barker, Dembo, and Lewin [3]. But these investigators never made entirely clear how general they regarded their definition of regression to be.

Therefore, although the experiment was ingenious and has been confirmed in large part (Wright, 1942), it also failed to generate a lot of controversy or followup research. As we shall presently see, there has been one relatively recent return to this problem by some psychologists, but by and large it has earned an honorable but uninfluential place in the history of the study of frustration.

The methodological criticisms alluded to above are two. First, the average I.Q. of their very small (N = 30) sample was 122. It has been questioned (Yates, 1962) whether their scale of constructiveness of play would necessarily generalize to a population of children at large. Second, and more important, the observations and ratings of play and other behavior throughout the experiment were done by people who knew the purpose of the experiment. There was no real control for the possibility that the raters' knowledge of the purpose of the experiment might influence their ratings. Of course, it could be argued that positive results in the face of this fact is even stronger support for the hypothesis. Experimenters sometimes bias their observations *against* the hypothesis in such situations in their attempts to be honest and objective.[3]

Once again we see the joint influence of Freud and common-sense notions about frustration being presented in a more formal and ostensibly more testable formulation. Once again we see the difficulties: Is there a general class of reactions that can be called regression? Is this an exhaustive description of the reactions to frustration that can be observed, and if not, what are the circumstances leading to alternative modes of reaction? And always there is the basic question, is one frustration situation the same as any other one with respect to the production of regression?

The Frustration-Fixation Hypothesis

Although the summarizing presentation of N. R. F. Maier's approach to frustration appeared later than the theories so far considered (Maier, 1949), the work on which it was based was going on during approximately the same period as those others. Far more important than its exact chronology, however, is the fact that it shared many characteristics in common with the other "early" theories, being heavily influenced by a common-sense appraisal of frustration and its effects.

Actually, the experimental work on which the theory was based, and by which the theory is properly judged, give Maier's approach a rigorous, formal appearance at first glance. But an examination of the elaboration of his viewpoint, as seen in the Readings, for instance, make it clear that Maier was definitely thinking of frustration as a "real-life" problem, for which his experimental program was only a limited model.

As with the frustration-aggression hypothesis in particular, Maier's theory aroused a great deal of controversy because of its rather sweeping statements concerning the effects of frustration. The subtitle of Maier's major treatise on the topic was "The Study of Behavior Without a Goal." His basic principle was that the behavior arising out of true frustration could not be explained in terms of conventional learning and motivational principles. This was just the opposite of the frustration-aggression hypothesis, for example, which was definitely rooted in one of the influential learning theories of the day. Maier stated to the contrary that the basic characteristic of

[3] See R. Rosenthal, "On the Social Psychology of the Psychological Experiment," *American Scientist*, 1963, **51**, 272.

behavior in a truly frustrating situation was that it became "fixated"; that this fixation did not arise because of ordinary reinforcement or motivational factors, and could not be changed by the therapeutic application of these factors. Fixated behavior, in short, was an end in itself and was to be considered entirely different from ordinary problem-solving behavior. In order to understand these rather extreme statements, we must pause to consider his basic experimental procedure and its most outstanding results.

Maier's research was done primarily with rats, using the Lashley jumping apparatus. This apparatus consists of a platform on which the rat is placed facing two windows on another platform. At the front of each window is a paper card, and each card is marked differently from the other. The rat is taught to jump from the starting platform to the other one. If it jumps at the correct window, the card falls down easily and the rat finds a food reward on the platform. If the jump is to the incorrect card or window, the card does not fall. Instead, the rat falls into a net a foot or so below the windows. The apparatus is appropriately shielded so that the rat is, for all practical purposes, forced always to jump at the windows.

As long as one card or window is consistently "correct" (that is, permits the rat access to food and prevents falling), rats learn such problems fairly readily. Maier's variation was to create, for his frustrated subjects, an insoluble problem; both the window and the card that were correct on a given trial were changed randomly so that no approach response could be consistently rewarded. Under such circumstances, as you might suspect, rats soon refuse to jump at all. So they were punished for refusing to respond. During the major period of this work a blast of air from behind was used to force a response; later this was changed to a sharp rap on the tail, because the air blast was found to be a very high-pitched whistle that caused unusual behavior ("audiogenic seizures") in and of itself. This, then, is Maier's operational definition of a frustration situation—one in which no adaptive, goal-oriented behavior can develop, but one in which the subject must continue to respond. It appears to be a much more severe definition of what constitutes a frustrating situation than most other theories use, but Maier began to equivocate about these requirements subsequently.

At any rate, within this particular situation, Maier made some remarkable observations. Rats subjected to the procedure outlined above developed very nonrandom patterns of responses in the situation. Most (around 80 per cent) began to jump always to one side, no matter what card was there; the remainder jumped always toward a particular card, no matter what the side. Remember that both of these strategies result in reward half the time and punishment half the time, as indeed would any other strategy. Of course, if we were to reward and punish on a consistent basis, similar behavior would emerge—rats would always jump to the side, or the card, that permitted access to food. So up to this point we cannot differentiate between adaptive and maladaptive behavior.

The interesting results occur when we change the solution. For the frustration group this means reintroducing a real solution; for the normally trained rats this means changing their former solution to another one. For simplicity, the typical procedure was to work with the position response (jumping always to one side) only. After frustrated and rewarded rats had developed a stereotyped response to one window consistently, this window is permanently locked and the opposite window permanently unlocked. Maier and his co-workers repeatedly observed that all of the normally trained rats would rapidly give up the formerly correct response and adopt the new one, but a sizable number of frustrated rats would not do so even after up to 200 trials. Now, these are all trials on which the subject is punished; nevertheless, they did not deviate from their original stereotyped response. This was called a *fixation* by Maier, and was regarded as the characteristic outcome of severe frustration.

Maier repeatedly asserted that a frustrating situation could not be defined by its observable features alone. Whether a situation was frustrating for a given subject could only be determined by observing whether fixated behavior developed. Once again we see a characteristic of some of the early frustration theories—a subtle kind of circularity in which the behavior purportedly being explained is used to define the existence of the variables that explain the behavior.

The outstanding characteristics of the fixated responses are as follows: (1) There seems to be an all-or-none quality to its development. Rats exposed to the frustrating situation and then to the soluble problem split into a bimodal distribution with regard to ability to learn the solution (for example, Maier and Klee, 1943). (2) Fixations can apparently be broken only by the technique of "guidance," which amounts to gently forcing the rat to jump opposite to its fixated preference. More standard learning methods were not found by Maier and his students to be effective. (3) Fixations are highly specific to the situation and the response involved during the frustration period. Allowing rats to walk a runway to the now-correct side did not break the jumping fixation (Feldman, 1953), and a fixated position habit in the jumping stand situation did not transfer to a maze situation.[4]

There is a great deal more detail than we can review here. Certainly, as Yates (1962) has said, Maier's empirical work has been unjustifiably played down by American psychologists interested in the experimental study of behavioral pathologies. The major reason for this would seem to be Maier's insistence that fixated behavior is governed by principles other than those that now constitute the basis of general behavior theory. There is a strong tendency for psychologists (as with all scientists) to seek the smallest number of integrating principles possible. Ever since Freud, psychologists have been enamored of the idea that even apparently maladaptive behavior was actually following adaptive principles. Because of these guiding assumptions, psychologists become rather peevish when it is suggested that certain phenomena require a separate explanation. Therefore the main issue of battle with regard to Maier's theory has been whether already established principles of learning and motivation can, in fact, account for his findings.

Basically, attempts to refute Maier's position have centered on two features of his standard experimental procedure: (1) the fact that jumping at least removes or avoids the punishment administered on the jumping stand (Farber, 1948; Wolpe, 1953), and (2) the fact that the insoluble problem actually involves an intermittent reinforcement procedure (50 per cent of stereotyped jumps *are* rewarded), which itself produces a very strong habit (Wilcoxon, 1952). Although these arguments are cogent, Maier (for example, 1956) has argued that neither of these counterarguments actually predicts the bimodal distribution for abandonment of the fixated response that he typically found. Furthermore, Maier considers it an advantage for the diagnosis and treatment of behavior pathology, rather than a disadvantage, to recognize that maladaptive behavior may either develop because of learning and motivation or as a fixation. Actually, however, Maier has had to reformulate and clarify his ideas somewhat (for example, 1956) just as have others who

[4] See Norman R. F. Maier, *Frustration* (New York: McGraw-Hill, 1949), 47.

took too dogmatic a position with respect to frustration and its effects.

Maier's critics have perhaps emphasized his two-factor heresy too much. Other problems with the theory, however, can be seen when viewed in the light of the orientation of this book. These problems arise in retranslating his laboratory findings into the context of real-life matters, something that Maier [4] is not averse to doing. When he turns to real-life matters, Maier takes the kinds of examples of frustration and reaction to frustration that most people would use. The match of such situations with his laboratory situation is sometimes difficult to see. An example that appears in many forms in his writings is the case of parents failing to show love and affection to a child. Common sense might lead us to agree that this could, indeed, be a frustrating situation for a child—but does it approximate Maier's operational definition of a frustrating situation? Maybe, but maybe not; it is hard to see the connection, and Maier does not clarify this difficulty.

Similarly, Maier has vacillated considerably on the response side, depending, apparently, on whether he was most influenced by his experimental findings or by real-life instances of reaction to frustration. When attending to the first anchoring point (the data), Maier seems very firm in regarding fixation of response as *the* criterion of frustration. But when he turns to a more vernacular description of frustration reactions, he concedes that fixation, aggression, regression, and resignation are *all* possible reactions to frustration (Maier, 1949), with anecdotal illustrations of true fixation notably sparse. At times he writes of the latter three categories as special cases of fixation; at other times he seems to treat them independently.

The reader should understand clearly that there is no *requirement* that a laboratory-based theory be easily translatable into vernacular or even clinical descriptions of frustration situations or frustration reactions. An alternative strategy would be simply to study the laboratory phenomenon exhaustively, including examination of its generality across a variety of laboratory procedures and kinds of subjects. This has been done on only a small scale in the case of Maier's theory (for example, Marquart, 1948). If it is a reliable and generalizable phenomenon, then it has a place in a scientific psychology. Its relationship to some vague concept from the natural language need, in fact, never become an issue. As things stand, however, Maier's work illustrates very well what can happen when one attempts to serve two masters, in this case the opposing languages of science and the layman.

FRUSTRATION INTEGRATED WITH GENERAL BEHAVIOR THEORY

The next stage in frustration theory development is marked by an increasingly technical view of the concept. This stage has several distinguishing characteristics: (1) An increasing emphasis on a wide variety of experimental work as the basis for theorizing, as opposed to a reliance on everyday examples of frustration and its effects. Some of the experimental work that takes on significance in the theories now to be considered was not even originally regarded as research on "frustration" by those who conducted it. (2) Coupled with a broader experimental base, these theories also attempted a closer alliance with more formal behavior theory. They were not mere appendages to such theory, but tried to show an integral interrelationship between frustration and general behavioral concepts. (3) Both of the above trends led to a reconceptualization of the frustrating situation itself. Instead of seeking a unique generic term or unique model for "frustrating situations," it came to be recognized that many kinds of already well-known independent variables could be involved. (4) This latter trend, in turn, brought a growing suspicion that there was no unique overt behavior characteristic of frustration situations. Instead, more basic changes in behavior—which could be manifested in many specific ways—were suggested as the outcomes of frustration situations.

All of these "trends" were, of course, anticipated in the frustration theories already considered as representative of the earlier period. I am not suggesting that there was any dramatic revolution in thinking, because science rarely proceeds by the revolutionary method. Accordingly, there is no implication intended that steps in all of the directions just mentioned were not, in fact, attempted by the earlier theorists. The new generation of frustration theorists, however, brought these trends closer to fruition.

This increase in the successful departure from the vernacular conception of frustration has, of course, its historical determinants. As a greater variety of experimental work was done over the years, more could naturally be incorporated in the thinking about specific problems. Furthermore, the rise of a truly thorough attempt at a rigorous behavior theory by Hull and his followers provided a matrix into which specific, miniature theories could be incorporated. Finally, the increasing use of infrahuman subjects—especially the rat—for the study of a wide variety of psychological phenomena helped to shift attention away from everyday conceptions of frustration and its effects. It is difficult to regard much of the behavior of a rat in a straight runway as being either regressive or aggressive, for instance. Because the rat in the straight runway was the experimental model for much research on Hullian concepts, and because many apparently "frustrating" operations could be performed in this context, new terms for describing the behavioral outcomes of these operations had to develop.

Nevertheless, the theories now to be considered to exemplify the trend in scientific evolution described in Chapter I: a phenomenon originally observed outside of the laboratory and described in nontechnical terms was undergoing the transformations in meaning that direct scientific scrutiny must force upon such a phenomenon.

There are three theories of frustration that are prototypes of this stage of the conceptualization of that phenomenon: the viewpoints of Child and Waterhouse, Brown and Farber, and Amsel. These will not be discussed in strict chronological order of appearance in the literature. Instead, in the order named above these three treatments of frustration themselves constitute an orderly progression toward the final type of theorizing in this realm.

The Child and Waterhouse Revision of Frustration-Regression

Child and Waterhouse, two more workers at Yale University, took as their specific point of departure the previously discussed frustration-regression hypothesis of Barker, Dembo, and Lewin [3]. In their first paper (1952) they discussed in detail alternative explanations of the findings of the previous workers. Their main point was that to treat "regression," or lowered constructiveness of play, as the primary outcome of frustration was an oversimplification of the case. They considered "lowered constructiveness" to refer to some general characteristic of behavior as a whole and argued that it was unlikely that frustration could have such a pervasive yet singular effect.

Instead, they suggested that quality of performance with respect to rather specific acts be treated as the major dependent variable at issue in such experiments as the Barker, Dembo, and Lewin [3] study. Here, then, is one type òf departure from earlier approaches to frustration: frustration is not regarded as generating unique behavior but only changes with respect to the possible behavior controlled by the environment in which the frustration occurs.

In the 1952 paper and also in the paper that followed the next year (see Readings [5]), Child and Waterhouse also made the second major departure from "classical" frustration theory in that the mechanisms of behavior change following frustration were not considered to be unique, either. They identified two basic mechanisms: interfering responses aroused by the frustration situation or its emotional consequences, and changes in motivation. Both of these concepts—interference and change in drive—had long been discussed in psychological circles without any particular reference to frustration. So what Child and Waterhouse were essentially suggesting was that frustration does *not* refer to unique antecedent behavioral causes but only to special cases of well-known determinants.

Having accepted the fact that a theory of frustration is only a special case of the application of known psychological principles in general, they were then able to elaborate a lot of possible conditions under which behavior might either deteriorate or actually improve as a consequence of frustration. These are detailed in the selection in the Readings [5].

In brief, Child and Waterhouse argued that when goal-directed behavior is in some way interfered with—that is, the standard concept of frustration—motivation is changed, and also other responses are likely to occur. The effect of motivational change can be predicted only by knowing a great deal about the alternative behaviors possible for a given subject in a given situation, as well as the subject's past history. There is *no one mode* of reaction to frustration.

All frustration theorists are driven to this position eventually by the observable facts of everyday life, of course. But other theorists, taking one or another page from Freud's notebooks, had at least attempted to posit a *basic* mode of reaction. Then their problem, often handled very ingeniously, was to posit how variants of this basic form of reaction could arise. The major contribution of Child and Waterhouse, from the standpoint of the evolution of the concept of frustration, was to reject this strategy and substitute the viewpoint that frustration and its effects presented no unique phenomena or relationships when viewed in the context of behavior theory at large. This development had, of course, also been reflected in the writings of many of Maier's critics, because Maier stated more definitely than anyone else that frustration and its effects were truly unique. Most of Maier's critics, however, were not primarily concernd with the frustration aspects of the problem—emphasizing the punishment, anxiety, and partial reinforcement features of his situation. As we shall see, though, all of these problems came back to roost in the discussion of frustration per se.

The Brown and Farber Frustration Theory

An article by Brown and Farber of the State University of Iowa faculty actually antedated the Child and Waterhouse contribution slightly, but their approach really went somewhat further in the development of this particular viewpoint, so it is simpler to consider it at this stage in the discussion. This very stimulating article is reprinted in large part in the Readings section [6].

After a very erudite discussion of how emotions in general should be treated within a behavioristic framework (specifically, the framework primarily developed by Hull, for example, 1943b), Brown and Farber took the problem of frustration as a special case in point. Their major thesis was that frustration could be regarded as *a higher-order hypothetical construct.*

The differences between the concepts of hypothetical constructs and intervening variables were not gone into by Brown and Farber (see Chapter I). Basically they were referring to a concept that integrates several interrelationships between antecedents and behavioral consequents. If we find, to give a simple example, that increasing water deprivation affects certain aspects of behavior previously reinforced by water, and we find a similar relationship for food deprivation and food-reinforced behavior, we may find it profitable to give a generic name to all such relationships between nutritive deprivation and changes in behavior. It may even turn out, hopefully, that a common scale of measurement might be found for all relationships included in such a construct.[5]

Hullian theory has used hypothetical constructs quite extensively, and many of them (for example, "drive," "habit strength," "excitatory potential") have become part of many psychologists' language.

---

[5] For a brief, lucid, and sophisticated account of hypothetical constructs or intervening variables see N. E. Miller, Liberalization of basic S-R concepts: Extensions to conflict behavior, motivation and social learning. In S. Koch (Ed.) *Psychology: A Study of a Science* (New York: McGraw-Hill, 1959), 276–286.

Brown and Farber are two psychologists to whom such constructs are familiar and useful. Accordingly, they explored the possibility that frustration itself could be defined in terms of such constructs. Basically, their reasoning was similar to that of Child and Waterhouse, in that they started with the premise that when the tendency to perform a particular response is in some way interfered with, other tendencies to respond are aroused by this act of interference. One obvious example of an alternative mode of response would be a tendency *not* to repeat the response previously aroused and then interfered with ("inhibition of response"). Or, just as suggested by Child and Waterhouse, tendencies toward other kinds of responses could be aroused.

Note that in this respect, this account and the one just discussed are quite similar. They are both essentially abstract, recognizing that a wide variety of specific reaction tendencies could be aroused as a result of frustration (interference), and only a knowledge of the specific characteristics of the frustrating situation and the organism's past history could enable us to predict exactly what alternative response tendencies would occur and in what strength.

Frustration, then, according to Brown and Farber, is a conflict between two opposing response tendencies—one response tendency being the one originally evoked by the situation (presumably some kind of goal-response), the other being some alternative response aroused by the frustrating interfering conditions themselves. This conflict between opposing tendencies leads to whatever could be said to be the unique behavioral consequences of frustration. Because frustration is defined in terms of the relationship between two hypothetical constructs—the opposing response "tendencies"—frustration is a *higher-order* construct; it is defined in terms of first-order constructs (which can theoretically be related directly to observables).

The *effects* of this conflict between opposing response tendencies, as postulated by Brown and Farber, are also very similar in general nature to those posited by Child and Waterhouse. One effect, given a predominant emphasis by Brown and Farber, is an increase in drive. Frustration adds to the total motivation of the organism, and thus strengthens more whatever responses are already strong in the situation. Thus, for example, if the goal-directed response is far stronger than any other behavior in the situation, frustrating it may lead to its occurrence with even greater vigor. The second effect is to produce unique internal stimuli (which might be called "emotional," or "affective"). These stimuli, in turn, may be related to other responses not previously present in the situation. The relationship might be that of an unconditioned, conditioned, or discriminative stimulus.

So we see that the *effects* of the frustration-produced conflict are also described in the abstract. There is no attempt to posit an inevitable outcome of frustration. The specific behavioral effects will be determined by a number of factors—but factors, it must be remembered, that are presumably encompassed and understood by general behavior theory.

Stripped of its formal trappings, this approach is very similar to that of Child and Waterhouse, as has been repeatedly noted. But such an ignoring of its formal characteristics would be a distortion. The theory was actually a very impressive tour de force with regard to the extension of Hullian theory in a direction that had frequently been suggested, but not attempted, by others who extolled the merits of the hypothetical construct approach.

Nevertheless, the major importance of this theory in terms of the evolutionary development of the frustration concept that I am arguing for lies in the fact that it was another attempt to relate the vernacular concept *frustration* to general behavior theory and to strengthen its status as a technical term. Notice, however, that as this is accomplished, the term becomes more and more remote from its everyday meaning and from the early clinically oriented hypotheses about the phenomena. Notice further that these more rigorous formulations are not *inconsistent* with the cruder notions—they are simply more abstract.

Unfortunately, neither the Child and Waterhouse nor the Brown and Farber views of frustration has as yet been productive of specific research in much volume. One obvious reason for this is that they both imply that as our knowledge of the basic principles of concepts, such as habit-family hierarchies, drive, and conflict, improves in general, our progress toward an understanding of the effects of frustration *is* being directly increased. Therefore, why not continue to concentrate on these basic problem areas, rather than directing attention to "frustration" per se? Another particular reason in the case of the Brown and Farber approach is that, for all its esthetic and logical appeal, the actual quantitative development of a Hullian type of theory is not sufficiently advanced to test some of their more detailed hypotheses. We cannot measure "excitatory potential" or "inhibitory potential" directly, and it is not certain that indirect measures (that is, measures of overt responding itself) should necessarily provide exact confirmation of hypotheses about the interaction of construct-based scales.

Presumably, of course, the very great amount of research on conflict itself from a behavioristic approach (see Miller, 1951, and Yates, 1962, for reviews) should have some bearing on the Brown and Farber hypothesis. But the conflict research has not emphasized the measures of the kinds of consequences of conflict that seem most relevant to the frustration version.

Amsel's "Frustrative Nonreward" Theory

One of the most recent, and still very active, theories of frustration is similar in some ways to that of Brown and Farber. This is probably no accident, because its proponent, Abram Amsel, did his graduate work at the University of Iowa, and undoubtedly was influenced by the efforts of Brown and Farber to deal with this concept.

The theories are similar in that both attempt to relate the frustration phenomenon specifically to Hullian theory. Amsel also uses the hypothetical construct approach, as did Brown and Farber, but Amsel's construct is different. Amsel's frustration construct is basically an addition to the concept of "fractional antedating reactions." Hull [6] and others had long used the notion that some perhaps unobservable component of responses to a goal (reinforcement) could be conditioned to other stimuli in the environment. These fractional goal responses themselves could then serve as stimuli or sources of motivation for the observable behavior. This theoretical device was intended especially to account for complex sequences of behavior in apparatus, such as straight runways and mazes. It was an attempt to preserve a complete S-R account of such behavior and avoid "purposive" or "cognitive" explanations. Not all psychologists are convinced that this particular theoretical twist accomplished all that was claimed for it, but Amsel is one who regards it as a useful device.

Amsel's particular contribution to this thinking was to elaborate the concept by adding the notion that nonreward caused a "frustra-

[6] C. L. Hull, *Principles of Behavior* (New York: Appleton-Century-Crofts, 1943), 100.

tion reaction," and fractional components of this reaction could likewise be conditioned to other stimuli in the environment. Thence the "fractional anticipatory frustration" could itself affect the observable behavior of the organism. This may seem like a modest advance in thinking, but actually it has many important implications—both for Hullian theory and, more important to the present account, for the evolution of frustration theory.

Amsel's unique contributions to the evolution of the frustration concept are two: (1) Only one basic operation is considered in this theory—nonreward after experience with reward. This is in distinct contrast to some of the elaborate lists of variables that can lead to frustration offered by other psychologists. (2) The anticipatory frustration concept is used as a basis for an explanation of some long-standing problems in the field of learning and motivation—the effect of intermittent reinforcement on resistance to extinction, and the occurrence of discrimination learning. Intermittent reinforcement, under most conditions, increases resistance to extinction as compared with continuous reinforcement. Discrimination learning—learning to perform a response in the presence of one stimulus and inhibit it in the presence of another similar stimulus—is likewise a readily demonstrable phenomenon. But adequate theoretical accounts of both of these phenomena are still lacking. Hullian theory had particular trouble in dealing with the intermittent reinforcement effect. Amsel believes, as you can see when you read his paper, that the difficulties in Hullian accounts of these two effects are much abated by recognizing that nonreward interspersed with reward has a frustrative effect.

This is not the place to get into a complicated comparison of the competing theories in these two areas of psychological research, although Amsel's paper gives a concise historical review of the problems. What is important to us at the moment is what has happened to the frustration concept itself.

Amsel himself questions whether he even has a "theory of frustration." [7] Certainly it is very different from the previous theories of frustration considered. In Amsel's treatment, a very restricted set of generalizations about the frustration concept is made. These are, in summary:

[7] Abram Amsel, "The Role of Frustrative Nonreward in Noncontinuous Reward Situations," *Psychological Bulletin*, 1958, **55**, 104.

1. Frustration is defined only with respect to nonrewarded trials interspersed with, or following, rewarded trials.

2. An anticipatory frustration reaction is conditioned to the environmental situation or specific stimuli in the environment.

3. This anticipatory frustration response in turn affects overt response strength in three ways: (1) by increasing over-all drive strength—that is, motivating immediately subsequent behavior; (2) by serving as a drive stimulus whose reduction may be reinforcing and to which other responses may be conditioned, and (3) by inhibiting overt behavior. In many superficial ways, then, Amsel is describing effects of frustration similar to those of many other theories, but his emphasis is different, as well as is the exact mechanism by which the effects occur.

More important than certain similarities and differences in Amsel's concept of frustration effects and mechanisms, however, is his goal in introducing the term. His ultimate aim is clearly to enable a modified form of Hullian theory to deal with some classic unsolved learning problems in an adequate systematic way. He is not at all concerned with the vernacular meanings of *frustration*. In his writings we find, for the first time in this field, a complete absence of references to anecdotal cases of frustration in everyday life. It is possible to argue, or course, that he might have gotten some hunches about the effects of frustration from a knowledge of everyday experiences, but this would be quibbling. Everyman's concept of frustration is now quite remote from the psychologist's.

Does this mean that Everyman's questions or hypotheses vis-à-vis what he calls frustration have been cast aside? Not necessarily. The aim of Amsel and other systematic theorists is to develop a clear, rigorous conceptualization of behavior and behavior mechanisms that would encompass any specific problems the layman might come up with, as well as some he might never think of. It is not the goal of behavior theory to deal only with esoteric events that occur nowhere except in the laboratory, but the refinement in language that comes from dealing with such problems is exactly where adequate behavior theory must start.

Amsel's theory is probably second in productivity of research only to the frustration-aggression hypothesis. Certainly of the "modern" frustration theories it has produced the greatest amount of empirical research. But, of course, part of its productivity is due to the fact that it is intimately tied in with general research problems that have concerned psychologists for years. This is all to the good.

Perhaps a question one might raise about Amsel's theory is why, in fact, he chose to stick with a concept that has such a past history of surplus and contradictory meanings. For the development of the present monograph, it is fortunate that he did so, because Amsel's work neatly caps off the next-to-last stage in the evolutionary conceptual process I am trying to illustrate.

"Frustration" Disappears, but the Problems Remain

As pointed out earlier in the text, the refinement of a vernacular concept into a scientific one sometimes leads to a disappearance of the original term. The problems intended to be coverd by the concept are more clearly pinpointed and put into the over-all perspective of the science. When the original descriptive term covers a wide variety of problems, it sometimes turns out that as these problems are solved, it is better to dispense with the descriptive term and substitute a new, neutral term with explanatory connotations. There has been one recent attempt to do this with respect to some of the issues frequently discussed in terms of *frustration*.

In 1962 two professors at Stanford published a book entitled *Deterrents and Reinforcement: The Psychology of Insufficient Reward.*[8] The major purpose of this work was to show how three classical problems in learning theory could be explained by one general principle, previously developed by Festinger (1957), called cognitive dissonance. A summary of the major contents of the Festinger and Lawrence work was given in an address by Festinger [8].

The learning problems covered were the facts that resistance to extinction is greater after intermittent rather than continuous reinforcement; after delayed rather than immediate reinforcement; and for a response of greater rather than less effort. These facts are true in spite of the fact that experimental subjects can be shown to *prefer* continuous, immediate reinforcement of a response requiring little effort. We have already seen, in discussing Amsel, that the intermittent reinforcement problem has been a chronic one. Although resistance to extinction as a function of previous delay of

---

[8] Douglas H. Lawrence and Leon Festinger, *Deterrents and Reinforcement: The Psychology of Insufficient Reward* (Stanford, Calif.: Stanford University Press, 1962).

reinforcement and as a function of effortfulness have not received so much attention, Lawrence and Festinger are correct in asserting that these relationships are also puzzles for the widely held basic premises of most learning theories.

What is important to note with respect to the present discussion is that all of the variables under consideration here constitute operations that psychologists have at one time or another called by the term *frustrating*. (See Chapter III.) Yet the only time Lawrence and Festinger use the term *frustration* is when they are specifically referring to Amsel's theory of intermittent reinforcement effects. In other words, some of the behavioral situations that laymen and psychologists started out by discussing in terms of frustration are now handled without any reference to that term. Another term, invented by a scientist to describe a general behavioral principle, has been substituted.

Now the theory of cognitive dissonance itself is very complex, and this is not the place to get into it too deeply. Basically, it proposes that organisms that are forced ("tricked," as Lawrence and Festinger sometimes say) into performing under less than optimal conditions find additional sources of motivation or reward for this behavior. There is a fair amount of data in support of this at the level of human behavior, especially verbal behavior (for example, Festinger, 1957). Lawrence and Festinger have ingeniously applied this principle to integrate and explain three seemingly disparate paradoxes in the field of classical learning theory. Even more ingeniously, or perhaps just boldly, they have gone so far as to assert that this principle is operative in a nonverbal organism, such as the rat, as it goes through its appointed rounds in mazes, runways, and so on.

Will the cognitive dissonance theory stand when applied to basic learning problems? It is too early to tell at this writing, and this is not the place for a critical evaluation of the theory. What is important, again, from the standpoint of our present concern is that it shows how problems originally stemming from a layman's concept of the world become increasingly refined in conceptualization until the layman's language may become essentially unnecessary. I am not asserting that Lawrence and Festinger have solved the problem of defining frustration. Their approach, however, does show one kind of solution that might occur.

I am also not trying to argue that the term *frustration must* disappear from a rigorous psychological language. But it can, and if it does not, then it will certainly come to have a more restricted, specific meaning, as in Amsel's work. This is in the natural process of things in the development of scientific language and scientific activity: we may start with "real" problems as the layman would define them. But these problems usually turn out to be too amorphous, too complex for adequate scientific analysis. To paraphrase a statement I have made before,[9] the purpose of scientific theory is not to recreate the superficial chaos of nature but to describe the specific underlying relationships involved in complex situations. If "frustration," as it occurs in the natural setting, has too many ramifications for a straightforward analysis—and many psychologists apparently are beginning to believe that it does—then the many relationships involved must be identified in more isolated contexts and perhaps even renamed.

[9] Reed Lawson, *Learning and Behavior* (New York: The Macmillan Company, 1960), 366.

CHAPTER III

Experimental Research on Frustration

ONE OF THE OFT-CITED VIRTUES OF THEORIZING IN psychology is that theories stimulate research (that is, are heuristic). This has, to some extent, been true in the field of frustration research. The frustration-aggression hypothesis, for instance, was particularly productive of research. Amsel's ideas too have generated a great many experiments, as has Rosenzweig's P-F test, which stems from his frustration theory.

Theories, even inadequate ones, are also sometimes used as a pedagogical aid. Even if there are several competing theories on a certain topic, they provide a set of focal points around which myriad experiments can be organized. Insofar as this helps the student to learn the data of a research area, all well and good, no matter what the ultimate fate of the particular theories involved. An excellent example of this mode of presentation in the field of frustration is to be found in Yates' *Frustration and Conflict*.[1]

I have by now been perhaps excessively redundant in pointing out that theories also make, or at least reflect, changes in the language of psychology.

[1] A. J. Yates, *Frustration and Conflict* (New York: John Wiley & Sons, 1962).

There is, however, another way in which theory is sometimes regarded. That is as a synthesis of a body of already available data on a topic. To oversimplify a bit, this view holds that theory to a large extent comes after the data, instead of starting from only a small empirical base and suggesting the kinds of data that need to be collected. This point of view is slowly gaining ground in psychology, although there are those who will challenge it vigorously.

Actually, this is certainly no either-or proposition. Data and theory, in practice, interplay with each other. Recent examples of this can be seen in the work of Amsel and of Lawrence and Festinger. Both of these approaches began with empirical problems, suggested a theoretical resolution, then proceeded to do more experiments to see if their suggestions were predictive.

The interplay is even far more complex than this. The work of one or many researchers may provide the stimulus for another psychologist to generate some form of theory. As in the above examples, this theorist and his students may proceed to test the theory empirically, but other researchers will also be stimulated by the theory, too. There is not an orderly sequence here, except when we oversimplify the historical events greatly. Also, theories long past the prime of their historical (evolutionary) importance may continue to generate occasional research, because experimenters get their ideas from many sources. There have been fairly recent studies of frustration-aggression (for example, Berkowitz, 1960), frustration-regression (for example, Block and Martin, 1955), and frustration-fixation (Staats, 1959), although according to the analysis of Chapter II all of these theories had much earlier passed their peak periods of interest to psychologists.

From the point of view of this monograph, however, I think it may be useful to deal with empirical research on frustration somewhat removed from theoretical contexts. Our primary concern is to see how an everyday word is translated into a technical concept. Theory certainly plays an important role in this process, as Chapter II attempted to document in some detail. But in an empirical science, words must ultimately be translated into action, too. When we set out to "study frustration" in the laboratory, we must perform some specific experimental actions. When we wish to observe "reactions to frustration" in the laboratory, we must make some kinds of observations—preferably involving measurement—of behavior. All of this seems rather elementary—in the abstract. But when scientists really get down to cases they too are making a contribution to the refinement of vernacular terms by specifying the operations necessary for their laboratory study. So the orientation of this chapter will be to see what psychologists have actually done when they set about studying frustration empirically, and further to see what this has done to the term itself and its relation to other psychological concepts.

There will be no attempt at a chronological presentation of the following material, because such a pattern is hard to discern and would have many exceptions. This, I think, reflects the fact that even when an experiment is rooted in a particular theoretical position, the scientist may turn to some everyday instance of frustration as a model for his exact experimental procedure. The most obvious exception to this is the research done or stimulated by Amsel. As previously noted, his primary concern is with a small number of specific experimental situations, and he has least obviously borrowed from everyday conceptions of frustration.

Principal Independent Variables in Frustration Research

When we "frustrate an organism," we do something to it. This "doing something," if the point has not already been made clear, is technically called the manipulation of some independent variable. So the logical starting place is to review the classes of independent variables that have been manipulated in experiments purporting to deal with frustration. The following list is adapted from a more technical review done by Professor M. H. Marx and myself a few years ago (Lawson and Marx, 1958a). Yates (1962) challenged this rather extensive list, saying that the definition of frustration must be made more succinct. I sympathize with his feelings, but there is little that can be done about this in a historical account. All of the following have in fact been suggested as frustrating operations, and it remains for further thought and research to decide which operations should be retained and which discarded as part of a definition of frustration.

1. NONREINFORCEMENT AFTER A HISTORY OF REINFORCEMENT. The prototype of this situation is simple extinction of an operant response. Because extinction of an operant showed so many of the same kinds of changes that occurred in the extinction of a Pavlovian

conditioned response, possible differences in the situations were overlooked for a great many years. In many cases of true Pavlovian conditioning, the nature of the UCS and of the CR itself would not lead us to think of Pavlovian extinction (withholding the UCS) as "frustrating." For example, extinction of the galvanic skin response, originally established by using electric shock as the UCS, would not be called frustration. But in instrumental responding the reinforcer is typically what we would call a "reward." Beginning in the 1930's it was common to find "frustration" and "simple extinction" used as interchangeable terms. Miller and Stevenson (1936) and Miller and Miles (1936) both reported on "emotional" behavior in rats during extinction of a runway response.

As noted in Chapter II, the growing belief that nonreinforcement after a history of reinforcement does not simply weaken the response involved has led to attempts to explain such phenomena as the partial reinforcement effect in terms of the operation of a frustration effect. The importance of frustrating effects with nonreinforcement has also been extended to the analysis of discrimination learning.

An interesting variant of the use of nonreinforcement as a frustrating condition has been exploited by Amsel (for example, Amsel and Roussel, 1952). This is a two-stage runway (sometimes a T maze) where initially reinforcement is available at the end of each stage. Then reinforcements are no longer given after the initial response. This procedure permits the experimenter to examine the changes in both the behavior being frustrated and the behavior following frustration. The resulting experiments have enabled Amsel to offer much evidence for his "three-ply" effect of frustration (motivating, stimulus, and inhibiting), although some of his claims for a discriminative stimulus effect of frustration have been questioned (for example, Tyler, Marx, and Collier, 1959).

Most of the research specifically relating the frustration concept to extinction or nonreinforcement has been done in what both Zeaman (1959) and I (1960) have called the "controlled operant" situation. This is the instrumental situation in which responses occur on discrete trials, the spacing of which is determined by the experimenter. Students of the free operant situation (of which lever pressing is the prototype) tend to avoid the use of concepts such as frustration. By and large they also have a very restricted definition of *emotionality* in general. But in looking at cumulative records of extinction sessions (for example, Ferster and Skinner, 1957), it is tempting to infer some sort of excitability during the early stages of such sessions.

2. PREVENTING COMPLETION OF A REINFORCED RESPONSE SEQUENCE. An example of this situation would be to train a rat to run down a runway into a goal box containing food, then place a barrier in front of the goal box. This is quite similar to extinction, of course, except that the subject is never exposed to the goal situation on the critical trials. A representative study of this procedure was done by Williams and Williams (1943). Most of the results are consistent with the principles of general behavior theory. Responses so blocked become weaker, and do so at a faster rate than under conditions of ordinary extinction. This is presumably because the strongest members of the response chain (entering goal box, searching for food) do not occur at all.

This procedure has not been studied extensively, and there are only a few studies in which it has been related to the concept of frustration. Haslerud (1938) studied chimpanzees, in whom evidence of emotionality is more easily observed than in rats, in a response-blocking situation. He found that the animals did show overt signs of disturbance, and this was more pronounced in younger animals.

3. PREVENTING A RESPONSE AROUSED BY GOAL STIMULI. This is closely related to the preceding kind of variable. However, in this case the previous reinforcer is within the subject's immediate environment but is inaccessible. In common parlance this would be called teasing. Finch (1942) studied this procedure extensively in chimpanzees with provocative results, getting many signs of "emotionality." The rat, however, has not supported the notion that this condition is frustrating or aversive. Both Schlosberg and Pratt (1956) and Lawson and Marx (1958b) showed that inaccessible food in a maze acted primarily as a secondary reinforcer. Of course, the classic use of this method as a frustration technique was by Barker, Dembo, and Lewin [3],[2] as discussed in Chapter II and reported in their own words in the Reading.

4. DELAYED REINFORCEMENT. When used as a "frustrator," the typical procedure is to train a subject under immediate reinforcement conditions and then introduce a delay. This can be done by delaying delivery of reinforcement once a response has been made (for example, Screven and Nunis, 1955), or by temporarily inter-

[2] Bracketed numbers refer to readings in Part Two.

rupting an ongoing response sequence (for example, Geier and Tolman, 1943). The latter technique is somewhat similar to Amsel's two-stage response procedure and shows somewhat similar effects. In the former case, evidence of "increased vigor" is often found.

5. CHANGES IN INCENTIVE CONDITIONS. Years ago Tinklepaugh (1928) reported in a rather anecdotal fashion that chimpanzees given lettuce under circumstances where they typically got banana would show emotional behavior, although under other conditions they would accept lettuce quite readily. Several years later, Crespi (1944) found that when rats repeatedly given a large amount of food for traversing a runway were shifted to a very small amount, their performance dropped markedly below that of rats trained from the beginning on the small portion. He interpreted this as an indication of an emotional effect of the shift in incentive amount. Zeaman (1949) offered weak support for this finding, weak perhaps because the difference in the amounts of food he used was much less than in the Crespi study. It is worth noting in passing that this Crespi-Zeaman effect was one of the findings that began to force Hullian theory to acknowledge that nonreinforcement had other qualities than merely the capacity to weaken a response. This trend, as we saw in Chapter II, is still going on in the work of men such as Amsel.

6. FAILURE. Most of the studies and procedures reviewed so far have involved the manipulation of what are sometimes called primary reinforcers. Let us turn now to the case in which the subject is prevented in some way from obtaining secondary reinforcers— that is, stimuli not inherently reinforcing but that have become so through association with still other reinforcers. All of this work has been done with human subjects, just as most of the primary reinforcement work was done with animals (whose conditions of primary deprivation are more easily controlled).

As a generic term, *failure* has little more to recommend it than does frustration, as far as precision goes. Failure, as it has pretty consistently been used in the psychological literature, refers to cases in which secondary or generalized reinforcers are withheld under conditions where they have been given before, or could possibly be given. The secondary reinforcers include such things as the approval of the experimenter, successful achievement of standards set by the experimenter or by the subject himself, or in some cases the attainment of some token reward. At the same time that these secondary rewards are not obtained for responding there may be an accompanying aversive stimulus—disapproval expressed by the subject himself or by another person (for example, the experimenter). In the vernacular, of course, failure has many more shades of meaning than just described, but psychologists have adhered fairly closely to the operations mentioned.

Failure, involving as it does secondary reinforcers, depends on a long history of prior learning by the subject. Within the subculture of school and college students who serve in most of these experiments, however, there is a sufficient common core of secondary reinforcers to make some of these experiments reasonably successful.

In general behavior theory, primary and secondary reinforcers are believed to have essentially similar effects. Accordingly, preventing the subject from attaining secondary reinforcers should have about the same effects as observed with primary reinforcers. To a great extent this is true, but not entirely. There is much more variability in the results of frustration experiments using secondary reinforcers. This is probably due to several reasons. Success versus failure experiments are frequently not as well designed as the corresponding animal studies; human subjects undoubtedly have a greater range of alternative behaviors with respect to failure than a laboratory rat has in regard to not being able to get food, and the problems of controlling both the subject's motivational conditions and the incentive value of the secondary reinforcers employed are much greater.

Nevertheless, many similar effects are observed with failure: there is often a tendency for a subject to increase his effort after failure, to try a variety of alternative responses, to show some kinds of emotionality (although the social nature of most failure experiments certainly restricts these somewhat), and eventually to abandon responses that continually end in failure. These results are about the same whether the subject first succeeds on the task being studied and then fails or if success is only implied by the experimenter's instructions but never accomplished by the subject.

An interesting aspect of the research on failure that could do with more study has been the investigation of methods of removing the effects of previous failure. The standard design is to have subjects fail repeatedly on some simple task (by falsifying their scores or setting impossible norms against which they are asked to compete), then have some sort of interpolated "therapy," then have the subjects resume the original task (for example, McClelland and Apicella, 1947; Rohrer, 1949; Sears, 1937b; and Smoot and Lawson, 1962). The procedure most effective in raising performance on the retest has been to give the subject success experience on a different task during the interpolated period. Rest—just getting away from the failure task for a brief period—also has a facilitative effect. This latter finding perhaps suggests that the effects of failure are not entirely affective but are also in part simple ("nonfrustrating") extinction effects. Surprisingly, reassuring the subject about his failure, or even explicitly telling the subject that his performance was falsified to make it seem poorer than it was (Smoot and Lawson, 1962), does not lead to much subsequent improvement. The range of interpolated variables studied, however, has been small; to use an old cliché, further research is necessary.

One aspect of failure that has not been studied in humans is the effect of repeated failure in a variety of situations. This would obviously be very difficult research to conduct, but it is of great relevance to many clinical and personality theories.

7. HYPOTHETICAL FRUSTRATING SITUATIONS. One way of studying frustration reactions that has perhaps been used more often than it merits is to present subjects with hypothetical frustrating situations and get their verbal reactions. The Rosenzweig P-F test (Rosenzweig, 1945a, 1950) is a prototype, and probably the best known of these devices. Subjects are shown line drawings of people being frustrated in a variety of ways. The subject's task is to give a brief verbal retort of the sort that the frustrated person in the picture might make.

This kind of research is working on a different facet of the problem than we have found in most of the material covered so far. There is a search here for personality characteristics of the individual tested and sometimes for typical trends in certain special groups of people. These tests, although they define presumed characteristics of frustration situations, are not really an independent variable in the strict sense of the term.

8. OTHER SUGGESTED VARIABLES. Two other kinds of operations, which are usually treated as separate topics in writing about psychology, could be considered to have elements of frustration in them as well, using the vernacular concept of frustration. One is punishment, the other is conflict.

A response that is punished is typically suppressed, at least for a time. If the suppressed response was the only means to a particular kind of reinforcement for which the subject is highly motivated, then the punishment itself could be considered as a frustrating barrier. Furthermore, a response that has both positive and negative tendencies toward performance is one very good definition of conflict. So we might say that conflict itself can be frustrating. Brown and Farber, remember, considered conflict the essential feature of frustration.

All of this may sound like playing with words. It is, and it serves very nicely to point up the fact that specific, operational definitions have advantages that global, vernacular terms do not. When we begin to dissect the term *frustration* into the variety of operations covered by that term we find many useful, specifiable variables. Perhaps the term *frustration* is superfluous as a description of antecedent conditions.

Obviously, however, there is a common element to all of the specific independent variables discussed. A response is strengthened by means of a particular program of reinforcement; then in one of a number of ways it is arranged that this response will no longer obtain that reinforcement (nor, in most cases, will any other response that is available to the subject in the situation). This is why it is tempting to try to define frustration as a barrier to a goal, response blocking, and so on. But this implicit allusion to some sort of physical barrier is only metaphorically correct in many instances. Furthermore, it still remains to be seen definitely whether the differences in reactions to these specific manipulations are more or less important than the similarities. It is easy to overemphasize either differences or similarities in phenomena.

PRINCIPAL DEPENDENT VARIABLES IN FRUSTRATION RESEARCH

The kinds of behavioral observations typically made in frustration research have already been hinted at throughout the preceding material, but it will do well to review and summarize them. Literally, the same dependent variables are used in this area as in any other kind of psychological research. What we are now looking for are phenomena akin to the problem of reward and nonreward discussed by Festinger in his article in this book. Most frustration procedures boil down to some kind of nonreinforcement or less effective reinforcement. It is axiomatic, therefore, that these procedures should all weaken the response that precedes any of them. This turns out, in most cases, ultimately to be true. But what else happens? Are there other behavioral manifestations, even if transient, that suggest that something more than mere response weakening is taking place?

1. CHANGES IN THE FRUSTRATED RESPONSE ITSELF. One effect on the frustrated response itself that has impressed many psychologists is that responses immediately after frustration may not begin to weaken right away but instead become stronger. This is the "increased vigor" phenomenon. This may be manifested in many ways —increased speed of responding, increased force of responding, increased concentration on a complex task. It has repeatedly, though not invariably, been observed. Why this is so has not been definitely established yet. Some psychologists suspect it is a reflection of prior learning—a more effortful response frequently accomplishes what a less effortful one will not; there is a marked tendency for organisms to expend the least energy necessary to obtain reinforcement, and only when reinforcement is no longer forthcoming do stronger versions of the response emerge. Other psychologists (for example, Amsel, 1951; Brown and Farber, [6]) believe that this increased vigor is due to an increased motivation caused by the frustration itself. Whichever turns out to be the case, this is definitely a temporary effect. Progressive weakening of the response eventually becomes characteristic.

Behavior sometimes becomes more variable in strength from trial to trial or moment to moment. In other words, the weakening due to nonreinforcement is not monotonic. This is sometimes regarded as evidence of the interference of competing, perhaps emotional, responses due to frustration. This matter is discussed in detail in the Readings from Brown and Farber [6] and Child and Waterhouse [5].

2. RESUMPTION, MEMORY, AND ATTRACTIVENESS OF FRUSTRATED BEHAVIOR. In all of these cases an answer is being sought to the question, does behavior (or the environment in which the behavior occurs) become aversive as a result of frustration? A positive answer is implicit in attempts to deal with discrimination learning in terms of frustration. And it has repeatedly been shown in the two-stage type of apparatus that rats approach the point of frustration

slowly and tend to leave it rapidly. Nevertheless, at the human level, no clear-cut answer emerges.

Three principal ways of asking the question have been tried. First, after success on some tasks and failure on others the subjects may be asked to rate the "attractiveness" of the tasks in some way. These results are probably least ambiguous; subjects generally rate successful tasks higher than ones on which they were unsuccessful. Second, after the same sort of procedure the subjects may later be confronted with a choice of resuming either tasks on which they experienced success or ones on which they failed. Here the picture is more complex. Rosenzweig (1945b) has argued that this behavior reflects a person's degree of frustration tolerance, a sign of maturity; in other words, mature people tend more to return to the tasks on which they have previously failed. There is much conflicting evidence on this point, however. Finally, memory for successful and unsuccessful endeavors has been studied. It is widely believed (not necessarily by psychologists) that we tend to remember the "pleasant" and forget the "unpleasant." Ideas of this sort are certainly at the bottom of the concept of repression, for instance. Proving the point experimentally, however, has turned out to be extremely difficult. With respect to memory of specific success and failure experiences in the laboratory, the evidence is simply not consistent at all. This research has been reviewed in more detail by Lawson and Marx.[3] In sum, it is safe to say that frustration is not the only variable operating with respect to these response tendencies.

3. EFFECTS OF FRUSTRATION ON NONFRUSTRATED BEHAVIOR. Also of interest is the effect that frustration may have on other behavior immediately following, but in no way involved with, the occurrence of frustration. The effects are generally deleterious with respect to perception and problem solving. There is an indication, however, that "increased vigor" sometimes operates in this case, too. Following failure on one task, subjects may try harder on a subsequent though different one (Postman and Bruner, 1948).

Certainly related to this matter is the regressive tendency found by Barker, Dembo, and Lewin [3]. As previously noted, Child and Waterhouse (1952) have suggested that this effect of frustration is due to the generation of competing responses, either conditioned or unconditioned.

[3] Reed Lawson and M. H. Marx, "Frustration: Theory and Experiment," *Genetic Psychology Monographs,* 1958, 57, 443–447.

4. FANTASY BEHAVIOR FOLLOWING FRUSTRATION. Do subjects with a history of frustration, or ones exposed to a specific frustrating situation, show any particular trends in their verbal fantasies to projective test materials? The available evidence is that they do. The changes may be of two types: an increase in aggressive fantasy (Yarrow, 1948) or an increase in "punishment expectancy" (Crandall, 1951). In terms of long-term history, however, an important variable in determining fantasy aggression is the degree to which real-life aggression (for whatever reason) has been punished (Hollenberg and Sperry, 1951); the less chance for real aggression, the more the tendency to fantasy aggression.

5. "EMOTIONALITY." As we study organisms higher than the rat, in whom only the most extreme forms of "emotion" are easily inferred from its behavior, we very often observe emotional behavior after frustration. Aggression, of course, is the emotional consequence most frequently noted, but as our discussion of Dollard *et al.* indicated, there is no simple relationship between aggression and frustration. An experiment by Finch (1942) is very enlightening here—"purely emotional" behavior seems to emerge primarily after all adaptive responses to the frustrating situation have been exhausted. As Lawson and Marx (1958a) suggested, this may have much to do with the commonplace observation that children react more emotionally to frustration than do adults—they simply have fewer adaptive responses available in the face of many frustrations.

Two very interesting studies bearing on the expression of emotion after frustration deserve special mention. Keister and Updegraff (1937) found that after using the method of successive approximations and a set of problems graduated so that the subjects could handle each new one with success, children who initially reacted to frustration with much emotional behavior become far less emotional and more adaptive in the face of unsolvable problems. Davitz (1952) showed that children permitted to behave aggressively in a particular environment showed a great deal of aggression after frustration, whereas children trained to behave quietly and cooperatively in the same environment (aggression was not punished specifically) showed very little aggression after the same sort of frustration. The hypothesis that some emotional responses are basically unconditioned forms of behavior that can be automatically elicited by certain UCSs (such as frustration) clearly needs a great deal of qualification.

Summary of Frustration-Oriented Research

The empirical delineation of the term *frustration* must still leave us in doubt as to whether it is useful as long as it retains the flavor of the vernacular. On the independent variable side, we can break the term down into several specific operations, some of which have only superficial commonalities with others. Insofar as a concern with "frustration" has led to a clearer perception of the complex nature of nonreinforcement (that is, that it is not just a passive weakener of a specific response) something has been gained in behavioral thinking. But the concept of frustration itself is not advanced by such an analysis.

On the dependent variable side, even ignoring operational differences in the antecedents, trying to find characteristic reactions to frustration has so far been largely unrewarding. Some kinds of reactions (emotionality, increased vigor) occur with a tantalizing frequency, but their occurrence can be manipulated by a variety of other factors as well.

It would seem that the apparently straightforward questions "What is frustration?" and "What are people's reactions to frustration?" are not straightforward at all. The best answers to these questions may not come from a frontal assault but by developing more technical questions capable of direct answers, even though the answers themselves may be highly technical.

Recently Discovered Phenomena Relevant to Frustration

A student familiar with the fields of learning and motivation will have recognized that in the section above on independent variables in frustration research I covered many of the conventional variables of those fields. Sometimes these variables have been studied in the context of frustration, and sometimes they have not. In recent years, some new independent variables affecting behavior in "learning" situations have begun to be studied. These variables seem to have some relationship to the topic of frustration, but it is interesting to note that the psychologists studying these phenomena have never seen fit to point this out. These relatively new areas of research, then, perhaps reflect the same trend at the empirical level that I suggested as occurring at the theoretical level—a shift away from frustration per se toward an examination of the related issues in terms of more technically defined dimensions.

Let us look, for purposes of illustration, at two such phenomena: "time out" and "behavioral contrast." Both of these have been studied for the most part in the free-operant situation, but seem to have analogues in other types of learning situations.

Time Out

This is a shorthand name for "time out from positive reinforcement." It is a period, in the free-operant situation, during which the subject cannot obtain any reinforcements for responding. When using the pigeon, a common subject in free-operant research, the procedure is very simple—all the apparatus, including the light in the experimental chamber, is turned off. The pigeon's normal behavior in total darkness is to roost, so its immediate reaction is to stop responding. With other subjects, extinction of responding must take place in the presence of the time-out condition, so this condition is functionally equivalent to a negative discriminative stimulus (S^Δ in free-operant terminology). In either case (automatic or learned reaction to time out), many of the effects are the same.

Originally, this technique was employed (especially with the pigeon) as an essentially "neutral" condition to separate successive periods of reinforced responding (for example, Ferster and Skinner, 1957). Later, however, the negative or aversive properties of this procedure began to be recognized. Ferster (1958) found that if a signal was presented shortly before time outs were programed, animals would react to this "warning signal" very much as they did in a standard avoidance conditioning situation—that is, they could be taught to respond in such a way as to terminate the warning signal and prevent the occurrence of time out.

In another example [4] of the aversive nature of time out, the procedure was used to sharpen a four-choice discrimination in the pigeon. The pigeon had to match one of four differentially marked keys to a display above the keys. Now, if the pigeon simply pecked the same key every time, regardless of the stimulus display, it would be reinforced on an average of once every four times. This is not a bad payoff for a pigeon in this situation; pigeons will peck at a high rate even when the average number of responses required per

[4] See B. F. Skinner, *Verbal Behavior* (New York: Appleton-Century-Crofts, 1957), 372–373.

reinforcement is in the hundreds. In order to prevent the pigeon from developing this one-key response and sharpen stimulus control, every incorrect match produced a brief time out. With the addition of this feature, accurate matching developed. Skinner explicitly refers to this use of time out as a "mild punishment."

Notice that the preceding experiments on the aversive properties of time out from reinforcement coincide nicely with the frustration analysis of discrimination learning put forth by Amsel. However, students of the time-out effect have never referred to frustration in their work, apparently feeling that it adds nothing to the account.

To show how complicated the analysis of behavior may become, and how little help vernacular terms may be, it may be profitable to digress a bit and discuss an anomaly found in the case of time out. Azrin (1961) placed pigeons in a two-key apparatus in which one key produced reinforcements on a fixed-ratio schedule (a fixed number of pecks was required before reinforcement would be given). A peck on the other key produced a time out that lasted until a second peck was made on the same key, restoring the conditions under which reinforcement could occur. Thus the pigeon could time itself out and could control the duration of the time out. In view of the preceding results, would a pigeon ever do this? It turns out that a pigeon will, and the frequency with which it does so is directly related to the size of the ratio (amount of work) required per reinforcement. Under large ratios (for example, 200:1) the pigeon frequently timed itself out. To oversimplify things a bit, the time outs in this case seemed to provide "relief" from a very demanding reinforcement situation.

Azrin's study simply illustrates the relativity of such terms as *aversive, punishing,* and *frustrating.* He has shown (Holz and Azrin, 1961) that even the effects of electric shock as a punisher are relative to other contingencies in the situation. In that study, severe shocks were always followed by the opportunity for reinforcement, whereas very weak shocks were never followed immediately by reinforcement. Under these conditions, severe shocks *facilitated* responding, whereas weak shocks came to suppress it (the typical effect of punishment), even though the weak shocks originally did not affect behavior.

All of this digression has been by way of showing that such vernacular terms as *punishment* and *frustration,* in addition to being vague, do not necessarily point out the complexities of behavioral control. It is not surprising, therefore, to find much research proceeding without reference to frustration, although the operations involved may have been so named in the past. Parenthetically it might be noted that the preceding discussion raises similar questions about the usefulness of the term *punishment*, another prescientific concept around which a confusing conglomeration of hypotheses and assertions centers.

Let us return now, however, to another frustrationlike phenomenon that has been investigated recently.

Behavioral Contrast

This phenomenon has been most extensively studied by G. S. Reynolds (for example, 1961), although he notes that it had been reported (under various names) since the days of Pavlov. The basic technique for demonstrating contrast in the free-operant situation is first to train a pigeon to peck a key when the key is sometimes red and sometimes green (equal durations of each). During initial training the rate of reinforcement under both colors is the same, so that the rate of responding in the presence of each color is the same. After stable rates are achieved, the frequency of reinforcement in the presence of one stimulus is markedly reduced; an extreme case would be the introduction of extinction, but changing rate of reinforcement, for example, from once a minute (on the average) to once every three minutes, has a similar effect. Of course, the rate in the presence of this stimulus drops correspondingly, but the interesting thing is what happens to behavior in the presence of the stimulus for which the reinforcement condition remains unchanged. The rate of responding to this stimulus *increases* over its former level, although none of the procedure in the presence of this stimulus has changed at all. This increase due to a change in the reinforcement conditions under another segment of the program is called "behavioral contrast."

Detailed experimental analysis of this phenomenon has shown that it is not an artifact of differential reinforcement of rate or inter-response times. The phenomenon would certainly seem to have some relation to a broad concept of frustration (the frustration being related to the component in which rate of reinforcement is reduced), though again there is no specific reference to this topic in any of Reynolds' work. A check for a simple "emotionality" effect (increase in general activity) has proved negative (Catania, 1961), in fact.

The operation of a contrast effect is presumably quite widespread, although rarely specifically noted by previous investigators. Reynolds has found in the research literature instances of a similar effect in discrete-trial discrimination experiments (both Pavlovian and "controlled operant"). Because it involves pitting an unfavorable reinforcement contingency against a more favorable one under different stimulus conditions, it could conceivably be called a new "frustration effect." But would this add anything to the account?

Other examples could be cited of relatively new behavioral discoveries that might be forced into the frustration mold. But the point is this: the investigators have not found it particularly useful to make such an affiliation. Instead, the identification of new dimensions of behavioral control is itself considered more important and useful. Thus, at the empirical as well as the theoretical level, the explanatory value of frustration is being viewed with increasing scepticism.

CHAPTER IV

The Future of Thinking and Research About Frustration

LET US CONCLUDE THIS ESSAY BY BRIEFLY REVIEWING the main themes that have been developed and what they suggest about the future of the frustration concept. I also wish to make a few remarks about areas of research on frustration that have not yet received much experimental attention.

As the review in Chapter III revealed, experimenters do not literally study *frustration*. They study the effects of delay of reinforcement, nonreinforcement, changes in incentives, physical blocking of learned responses, and so on. Some or all of these effects may have similarities that override the superficial operational differences in procedures. Lawrence and Festinger, for instance, have attempted to show such interrelationships for one behavioral measure—resistance to extinction. If such similarities are clearly established for a variety of response measures, then it may be satisfactory to call the basis of these similarities *frustration*. But this is quite a different matter than having an a priori conceptualization of the meaning of the term.

In Chapter I it was noted that a psychological concept may refer to any of three classes of events: (1) antecedent conditions, (2) behavioral consequents, or (3) a relationship—presumably explanatory in nature—between these first two classes. In other words, we may define *frustration* as what is done to an organism; we might define it as a unique form of behavior resulting from doing certain things to the organism, or we can attempt to use the term to explain relationships between a specific class of antecedents and class of consequent behaviors. As also noted, these three usages tend to become intermingled in many prescientific terms referring to psychological phenomena.

It is probably the role of frustration as an explanatory device that is most vulnerable, as we refine our terms in psychology. Terms whose meanings need only operational specification may persist, as can be seen in every science (for example, acid, length, volume). Prescientific terms with apparent explanatory capacities are usually the ones that disappear as we begin to understand more about the processes at issue in a specific case. However, in the particular case of frustration, its usage even in the first two ways mentioned above has difficulties simply because the term is used in too diverse a set of situations.

What will probably turn out to be the case is that some of the antecedent conditions reviewed in Chapter III will have similar effects, and some will not. Then psychologists will have to decide for which, if any, of the clusters of independent variables the term *frustration* should be retained.

An empirical search for "reactions to frustration" (that is, reactions to any of several independent variables) runs into the same problem. *Does* an individual person (or rat, or monkey) react to the numerous variables described in Chapter III in the same specific way? Superficially this seems virtually impossible. Writers such as Child and Waterhouse have tried to point out that the directly observable reactions to frustration must be a product not only of the "fact" of frustration but also of the other situational determinants present when the subject reacts. Dollard *et al.* have further discussed the historical determinants that may affect such behavior. So it would seem that hypotheses of the form "frustration always leads to . . ." must be so heavily qualified as to be questionable as far as reference to directly observable behavior is concerned.

Of course, the traditional attempt to rectify this difficulty has been to seek some higher-order description of the many specific reactions to frustrating operations. These higher-order descriptions, as noted in Chapter II, were originally qualitative (for example, "extrapunitive," "aggressive"). In later attempts, such as those of Brown and Farber, and Amsel, the trend was toward the identification of quantifiable behavioral changes. Increased vigor of responding, for instance, is quantifiable, and applicable to many behavioral situations, though not all.

There are those, such as Rosenzweig, who continue to seek to establish general, higher-order descriptions of behavior unique to frustration situations. So far, this work has been carried out primarily in the realm of personality theory. Direct lines of communication between personality theory and experimental psychology are still sparse and frail. This is no criticism of either camp, of course. Perhaps a mutual concern with such problems as frustration will lead to the mutual understanding and respect for one another's problems and methods that many psychologists hope for. From the standpoint of experimental psychology alone, however, the current inclination is away from broadly defined dependent variables (such as "extrapunitive behavior" or even "aggression") to more specific, measurable aspects of behavior.

All of this may discourage the young student of psychology (and even some professional psychologists), because of a reluctance to see apparently useful concepts disappear. The thesis of this book has been, in part, that this usefulness is *only* apparent. Usefulness here is being confused with familiarity, and the familiarity comes not from these concepts' success within a scientific psychology but from frequent vernacular and semivernacular usage. The point is that nothing is really being lost, and much is being gained. The disappearance, or more strict definition, of laymen's terms does not mean a loss of concern with the problems to which these terms vaguely allude. It simply means that a different vocabulary—and the attendant differences in the questions asked—will arise. Hopefully, this will lead to a more useful set of suggestions even for such things as certain kinds of psychotherapy. There is nothing new in all of this. One has only to read the history of medicine to see how the laymen's concept of disease and its treatment was left far behind as medicine developed a more scientific base.

In short, then, the fate of the concept of *frustration* as a technical term in psychology is largely the fate of the development of behavior theory in general. There is little doubt that a general behavior theory will not readily "make sense" to a layman, and the ultimate psychological usage of the term *frustration* probably will not either.

Returning to the vernacular concept of frustration for a moment, however, there are three problems concerning this broad term that have not yet been studied to any extent in the laboratory but which seem provocative.

First, there is the well-known hypothesis that early frustration affects behavior in later life—both with respect to later reactions to frustration and with respect to other aspects of behavior. This has only been studied in a very limited way experimentally, although clinical psychologists—following the lead of Freud—are often highly impressed with it. Nevertheless, as Orlansky (1949) and Beach and Jaynes (1954) have pointed out, experimental studies of the longitudinal effects of specific variables are sadly lacking in psychology. This is no surprise. They are very time-consuming and very difficult from a methodological standpoint.

Second, there is the question of "frustration tolerance." This is partially related to the preceding question, but put with a slightly more applied emphasis. The question is, what historical or situational factors lead to "frustration tolerance?" Again, except for an occasional provocative study such as those by Davitz (1952) and Keister and Updegraff (1937), little of a systematic nature has been done on this problem, which is of vital concern both practically and theoretically.

Finally, there is the again somewhat related problem of how to remove the undesirable behavioral consequences of a specific frustrating situation once they have occurred. This assumes that severe frustration can produce some sort of pathological behavior that persists beyond the mere removal of the frustrating condition. Actually, only Maier, among the psychologists we have covered, has presented evidence that might support this assumption. Maier has also suggested the only solution—his method of guidance. But it is difficult to generalize his procedure of gently pointing a rat by hand toward the appropriate window to a more broad program of therapy. Analogies may be drawn with respect to some educational techniques involving successive approximations, but it is not clear that the same mechanisms are really involved.

All of these questions, or some minor variants of them, may still strike you as reasonable questions to ask experimentally. But are they? The specific problems suggested by these questions are real problems, but if the viewpoint of this book is valid, can they be answered in the forms given?

To take one example, how many experiments would be needed to answer the question "What is the effect of early frustration on reactions to frustration at a later time?" The answer is, apparently, innumerable experiments, because we are still not sure that "frustration" is a thing in any sense, and we are even less certain that "reactions to frustration" are in any way constant for a given individual. Reducing this question to operational terms would require studying a multitude of specific "frustrating" operations, in both early and later developmental stages, and all of the combinations of these. To complete the picture, investigators would probably want to try more than one dependent variable measure as well. And on top of all this, there is the ubiquitous temporal variable itself: over what intervals of time should effects be traced? You can see why experimenters are not rushing into this area. But the obstacles of hard work or an extended program of research aside, the point I am trying to make is that the problem as phrased may be basically unanswerable, due to the nature of the term *frustration*.

All is not lost, however. The current developments in the refinement of the term, its integration with broader behavior theory (which is getting more to the point all the time), and the development of efficient research methodologies for studying long-term processes all give basis for hope. An understanding of basic behavior problems may come sooner than we think. By refining the basic issues involved we may be able to bring to bear a broad background of empirical knowledge against which a few, very penetrating experiments may reveal the essential principles about "frustration" that the questions listed above seek.

PART TWO

The Selected Readings

Important Sources Included in Whole Or in Part

[1] S. Rosenzweig, "A General Outline of Frustration"

[2] N. E. Miller (with R. R. Sears, O. H. Mowrer, L. W. Doob, and J. Dollard), "The Frustration-Aggression Hypothesis"

[3] R. G. Barker, T. Dembo, and K. Lewin, "Frustration and Regression"

[4] N. R. F. Maier and P. Ellen, "The Integrative Value of Concepts in Frustration Theory"

[5] I. L. Child and I. K. Waterhouse, "Frustration and the Quality of Performance: II. A Theoretical Statement"

[6] J. S. Brown and I. E. Farber, "Emotions Conceptualized as Intervening Variables—With Suggestions Toward a Theory of Frustration"

[7] A. Amsel, "Frustrative Nonreward in Partial Reinforcement and Discrimination Learning: Some Recent History and a Theoretical Extension"

[8] L. Festinger, "The Psychological Effects of Insufficient Rewards"

[1]
A General Outline of Frustration
SAUL ROSENZWEIG

TYPES OF FRUSTRATING SITUATIONS

If frustration is broadly defined as failure in biological adjustment, the first general question which arises in a systematic analysis of the phenomenon concerns the general classes of frustrating situations to which human beings may succumb. Three such broad classes may be distinguished—privations, deprivations, and conflicts—each of which may be further characterized as having its source without or within the individual. First, there is a type of frustrating situation in which the individual needs or wants some general object or end state which is ordinarily supplied by the external world but which is now not to be found there—general negative exogenous frustration or *external privation*. For example, a man on a desert island is sexually in a state of tension but no woman is available to him, or he is hungry but can find no food. In the second place may be distinguished a type of frustration in which the individual suffers not because some general property is lacking in the external world but rather in himself—general negative endogenous frustration or *internal privation*. A common example in the sexual sphere would be the situation of a person who has insufficient attractiveness for the satisfaction of his mating drive. Next are two types of frustrating situations which are also negative but in the sense of a rather specific loss rather than a general lack. One such situation is characterized by the loss of some environmental object or end-state to which strong specific attachments have been formed in the past—specific negative exogenous frustration or *external deprivation*. Thus, a man is deprived by death of the woman with whom he is in love, or the house he has lived in for many years is destroyed by fire. A

SOURCE: Saul Rosenzweig, "A General Outline of Frustration," *Character and Personality*, 1938, 7, 151–160. Reprinted by permission of Duke University Press and Saul Rosenzweig.

fourth situation involves the loss not of anything environmental but of some specific attribute formerly possessed by the individual and inextricably interwoven with his previous habits—specific negative endogenous frustration or *internal deprivation*. For instance Abelard is castrated by the jealous guardian of Heloise; Samson's hair is shorn and he loses his great strength. In the fifth place may be distinguished a type of frustrating situation in which it is not the absence of something in the external world but rather its unfortunate presence which tends to thwart the subject—positive exogenous frustration or *external conflict*. For instance, suffering from unsatisfied sexual cravings, a man meets an attractive woman only to find that she is the faithful wife of someone else. The presence of the marriage pact, representing social sanctions and regulations, stands in the way of satisfaction by arousing certain needs for security and integrity which conflict with the sexual needs. Sixth, and last, is a type of frustrating situation in which an obstacle is present in the individual's own personality by virtue of its organization which prevents the attainment of certain satisfactions—positive endogenous frustration or *internal conflict*. For example, a man is much attracted by a woman erotically but cannot find satisfaction because, whether with more or less consciousness she is identified in his mind with his mother or sister and thus arouses certain needs for integrity or security which conflict with sexual needs. In this class are found the sort of psychological conflict with which psychoanalysts are usually concerned; for instance, the so-called Oedipus complex. It should be noted in passing that both external and internal conflict situations are here regarded as varieties of frustration, but differ from privations and deprivations in that conflict involves the frustration of one need by another need.

It will be readily seen that, making due allowance for combinations, blends and transitional varieties of these "pure cultures," the foregoing types of frustrating situations are logically exhaustive. What is more, they seem also to be exhaustive psychobiologically. How true this is may be seen from the ease with which the various kinds of human unhappiness for which the aid of the psychiatrists is or should be sought may be assigned to these categories: the destitute (external privation or deprivation), the delinquent (external conflict), the defective (internal privation or deprivation), and the disordered (internal conflict).

FRUSTRATION TOLERANCE

The second natural question in an analysis of frustration may be put as follows: Given an individual in any one of the frustrating situations just described, with what degree of tolerance is he apt to meet it? A concept like frustration tolerance has long been implicit in the thinking of abnormal psychologists and of psychiatrists, but the explicit recognition of it would seem to have considerable value. With this purpose in mind frustration tolerance might as a first approximation be defined as the capacity of the individual to withstand a given frustrating situation without distorting the so-called "objective" facts of the life situation. One must recognize that the frustration tolerance of an individual need not exist at the same level throughout his personality; in other words, areas of low or high frustration tolerance may be hypothetically posited. Such an hypothesis might even provide a working definition of the difference between the psychotic—in whom a generalized low frustration tolerance would be said to obtain; the neurotic—in whom certain circumscribed areas of low frustration tolerance (complexes) might be posited; and the normal individual—in whom a relatively high frustration tolerance would usually be found throughout the personality.

Individuals presumably differ, either constitutionally or as a result of experience, in the possession of this capacity. It would be easy to make it plausible that the educational process in childhood, especially as related to discipline, consists largely in the building up of frustration tolerance or the encouragement of its natural maturation. Frustration tolerance appears to be fostered by allowing the child to experience small amounts of frustration—amounts which he can negotiate without reacting inadequately. Such optimal doses of frustration are probably indispensable as an incentive to learning of any kind. But if, on the one hand, less than this ideal amount of frustration is experienced over a long period of the individual's early life, insufficient frustration tolerance will be developed for meeting the frustrations of later years. Such persons are said to be immature because "spoiled" or overindulged.. If, on the other hand, the child is frustrated much beyond his resistance, areas of low frustration tolerance (complexes) may be created and the ground prepared for behavior disorders. The psychoanalysts have taken cognizance of some of these facts in describing a transition from the primary to the secondary functions or from the pleasure to the reality principles. However, the concept of frustration tolerance seems preferable because it is quantitative rather than dichotomous, and has definite implications for experimental measurement. Some day we may be able to report frustration tolerance quotients as we now attempt intellgience quotients. . . .

. . . Re-education or psychotherapy is readily interpreted as a process of building up frustration tolerance by allowing the patient, as in the psychoanalytic situation where frustrations are constantly discussed, to experience small or tolerable doses of frustration until resistance is gradually developed and the areas of low frustration tolerance disappear. The recent experiments of Keister and Updegraf (1937) are examples of such re-education.

A more critical definition of the concept of frustration tolerance emerges from the answer to the third and last general question which an analysis of frustration involves—the question as to the ways in which an individual may react to frustrating situations.

TYPES OF REACTION TO FRUSTRATION

Adequate–Inadequate

In discussing frustration tolerance it has been pointed out that reactions to frustration may differ in their degree of adequacy. The higher the frustration tolerance, the greater the presumed adequacy of the reaction. It now becomes necessary to define somewhat more exactly the criteria by which adequacy is to be evaluated.

One of these criteria is social in reference. From this standpoint a response is regarded as adequate in so far as it does not misrepresent the facts of the frustrating situation as understood by the majority of those individuals who are in a position to observe but are not involved in the frustration. An ideal substitute for such a consensus would be some one omniscient individual who views the situation in complete detachment. A criterion of this social sort is invoked in extreme instances for deciding whether a person should be committed to a mental hospital—whether, for example, he has hallucinations or delusions.

A second criterion centers attention upon the individual's behavior as such. According to this individual criterion, reactions are regarded as adequate in so far as they are progressive rather than retrogressive in implication. Responses which tend to bind the subject to his past unduly or which interfere with reactions in later situations are less adequate than those which leave the individual free to meet new situations as they occur. Retrogressive responses in a frustrating situation make for inappropriate reactions on later occasions.

Progressive behavior, on the other hand, favors the natural development of the individual in accordance with his own potentialities and with the demands of the environment as these arise.

An instance of an adequate reaction would be found in the countering of an argument against one's ideas by legitimate attempts to uphold one's views instead, say, of backing down through excessive fear of striking out inappropriately through rage. It should be clear that fear and rage are not always to be regarded as inadequate modes of response; sometimes they are well warranted by the facts of the environmental situation. While such emotion may in one sense interfere with effective adjustive response, it may in other respects, e. g., through appropriate autonomic mobilization, facilitate such behavior. Similarly it would not be an inadequate mode of response if a person who was starving suffered pangs of hunger due to stomach contractions—however much this might be a confession of physical inadequacy against environmental odds—because no inappropriate reaction would here be involved. If, on the other hand, a person suffering hunger began to blame someone in his social environment when the condition had arisen from factors over which this accused person had no control, and if this reaction were actually based upon the hungry person's low frustration tolerance—he might secretly feel it a reflection upon his capability that he had no food but might lack the ego-strength openly to accept this fact—then a truly inadequate reaction to frustration would be involved.

It hardly requires to be pointed out that from the biological standpoint even inadequate modes of response are to be regarded as adjustive in aim—the best of which the organism is capable under the existing conditions, internal as well as external. Presumably an attempt is being made even in cases of psychologically inadequate reaction to preserve integrated functioning by keeping the so-called "ego" intact or by re-establishing equilibrium through the satisfaction of perseverative needs. When these ends cannot be achieved in a psychologically more adequate way, less adequate ones are resorted to. Similarly the body in its resistance to infectious disease avails itself of nondisruptive protective reactions as long as this is possible but may eventually have to utilize defenses which as 'symptoms of the disease seriously interfere with the patient's normal behavior.

It should be recognized that the above criteria of adequacy require further definition. An important problem for research is here involved.

Direct–Indirect

A second question regarding reactions to frustration concerns their directness. Some responses are patterned after the frustrating situation in a relatively straightforward way, whereas others have in greater or lesser degree the character of a substitute. Such substitutes are sometimes easy to identify, but are often highly indirect and symbolic. Factors which make for the inhibition of the direct response at the same time prepare the ground for such substitute reactions. It is understandable that many inadequate modes of response to frustration will have such an indirect character. It is not to be overlooked, however, that many adequate reactions are also substitutive.

Defensive–Perseverative

A third important characteristic of reactions to frustration is concerned with their role in the economy of the organism. In some instances the response is defensive in nature; the integrity of the so-called "ego," the organization of the personality, is at stake and is protected. Such behavior has recently been subjected to a certain amount of experimental study (Rosenzweig, 1938a; Sears, 1936, 1937a). Other reactions to frustration are perseverative (perseverant or persistent) in character; they seem to have the function of obtaining ultimate gratification for frustrated needs in spite of the immediate impasse that may have been encountered.

Defensive reactions may, of course, be adequate or inadequate and direct or indirect. Examples of direct adequate and inadequate responses have already been given in the discussion of adequacy. An indirect adequate reaction of defense would, for instance, be involved if a person threatened by an armed burglar called upon the police for help instead of attempting to cope directly with the situation single-handed. Of much greater import, however, are the inadequate forms of indirect defense reaction. On the basis of certain observations elsewhere reported (Rosenzweig, 1935) such behavior in frustrating situations may be tentatively classified as follows: (1) Extrapunitive [1]—when the individual tends to blame the external world, reacts with anger and hostility, and psychologically defends himself by what the psychoanalyst describes as the mechanism of projection. An ego which fears blame from others thus protects itself by blaming others instead. The most striking examples of this type of reaction to frustration are found among paranoid patients. (2) Intropunitive—when the individual tends to blame himself, reacts with feelings of remorse and guilt, and employs the mechanisms of defense called by the analyst displacement, isolation, and undoing. An ego which fears blaming others thus gains security by blaming itself instead. Classical examples of this type of reaction are found among obsessional and compulsive neurotics. (3) Impunitive—when the individual tends to pass over frustrating situations lightly, as if they represented unavoidable accidents for which no one was to blame. Here the motive of conciliation predominates, and the commonest mechanisms of defense are self-deception and "repression." An ego which fears loss of love thus protects itself from alienation by refusing to blame anyone or anything, emphasizing the inevitable and the excusable instead. Examples of this type of reaction are most strikingly found among hysterical patients.

Besides these defensive types of reaction to frustration there are the perseverative ones already mentioned. Such reactions aim not so much at protection of the ego as at the ultimate satisfaction of the frustrated need in spite of the immediate frustrating circumstances. While the aim of the defensive responses is to preserve the integrated organization of the personality as a whole, perseverative reactions are more concerned with the consummation of particular drives. Behavior of the latter sort may be either directly or indirectly perseverative, i.e., the striving may be in the very terms of the frustrating situation or frustrated activity, or may be only secondarily or remotely related to these. Direct perseverative reactions may be

[1] The terms *extrapunitive, intropunitive,* and *impunitive* have been used and are here used to describe inadequate defense reactions. It must not, however, be forgotten that all of these inadequate responses have their adeaquate counterparts. It even seems desirable to employ the above terms generically instead of pre-empting them for the inadequate types of response. By this usage the reaction would be described not only as extrapunitive, for example, but also as adequately or inadequately so.

in the nature of persistent or perseverant goal-oriented behavior which has some possibility of success, in which case they are to be regarded as adequate; or they may resemble what Hamilton (1925, p. 251) has called "persistent nonadjustive reactions," in which case they are clearly inadequate. Indirect perseverative reactions to frustration, on the other hand, comprise what are often characterized as substitute modes of gratification. These may also be regarded from the point of view of their adequacy, particularly from the standpoint of the progressive-retrogressive or individual criterion. At the adequate end of such a continuum stands sublimation, as understood by the psychoanalysts, and at the inadequate end regression. Other substitute gratification mechanisms would fall somewhere between these two end-points. A number of experiments done in the setting of Lewin's psychology (1935) furnish concrete data in this connection. Some of David Levy's experiments on dogs (1934) and chickens (1938) are also pertinent here.

Specific–Nonspecific

There is a fourth important distinction to be noted among responses to frustration. In addition to the specific defensive and perseverative reactions already described, there are certain *nonspecific* ones. Nonspecific reactions to frustration, unlike specific ones, do not have a clearly elaborated symbolic relationship to the frustrating situation in question. They are more physiologically structural than psychologically dynamic in nature. They too may be described as defensive or perseverative, adequate or inadequate, direct or indirect. Instances of nonspecific, defensive direct reactions to frustration are perhaps found in the phenomena of fatigue, inhibition, and sleep as interpreted by Pavlov. The normal daily cycle of sleep and wakefulness may serve to illustrate the adequate types of such defensive reactions of the organism. When, as presumably occurs in neurasthenia, fatigue begins to be a substitutive reaction to frustration, the indirect and at the same time, in this instance, the inadequate modes of nonspecific response are exemplified.

Nonspecific perseverative direct reactions are illustrated by the phenomena of distraction and reduced efficiency which supervene upon frustration. A failure of inhibition is probably involved here, but the criteria of adequacy and inadequacy are not yet clear. Indirect reactions of this category may be said to occur when, for example, distractions are exploited as substitute outlets for frustrations in other spheres of activity. It is possible that an instance of such surrogate behavior of the inadequate sort underlies the impunitive reaction to frustration and if so one would here find an interesting coalescence of a nonspecific perseverative reaction with a specific defensive one.

The above description of reactions to frustration should not be construed as an attempt at formalistic classification. The four characteristics discussed are obviously not dependent upon each other in any categorical way, nor are they the only aspects that might have been accorded special treatment. We are just at the beginning of experimental research in the field of frustration, and the value of our classifications and analyses must ultimately be tested by controlled observation. If the preceding outline suggests problems for such research and gives at least a semblance of integration to the complexity of the factors with which we have to deal, it will have served its purpose.

In so far as success may in the future be achieved with the aid of the frustration formulation, the co-operation of psycho-pathological, especially psychoanalytic, principles with experimental methods should testify to it. From such a *rapprochement* the concepts of psychoanalysis ought to profit by new precision and consistency which will add to their rich connotation that greater definiteness of denotation so long desired by certain psychologists and psychiatrists. This reorientation should also benefit academic psychology by bringing within its purview problems which are of crucial importance in everyday life.

From an even broader perspective one might hope that a psychology of frustration would tend to lessen the artificial division which now separates normal from abnormal psychology, and abnormal psychology from theoretical psychiatry. Once psychopathologists begin to employ experimental methods as envisaged here and psychologists of the normal begin to deal seriously with problems other than sensation, perception, and rote learning, one common set of dynamic principles should naturally emerge.

[2]

The Frustration-Aggression Hypothesis

NEAL E. MILLER (with the collaboration of Robert R. Sears, O. H. Mowrer, Leonard W. Doob, and John Dollard)

The frustration-aggression hypothesis is an attempt to state a relationship believed to be important in many different fields of research. It is intended to suggest to the student of human nature that when he sees aggression he should turn a suspicious eye on possibilities that the organism or group is confronted with frustration; and that when he views interference with individual or group habits, he should be on the look-out for, among other things, aggression. This hypothesis is induced from commonsense observation, from clinical case histories, from a few experimental investigations, from sociological studies and from the results of anthropological field work. The systematic formulation of this hypothesis enables one to call sharp attention to certain common characteristics in a number of observations from all of these historically distinct fields of knowledge and thus to take one modest first step toward the unification of these fields.

A number of tentative statements about the frustration-aggression hypothesis have recently been made by us in a book (Dollard *et al.*, 1939). Unfortunately one of these statements, which was conspicuous because it appeared on the first page, was unclear and misleading as has been objectively demonstrated by the behavior of reviewers and other readers. In order to avoid any further confusion it seems advisable to rephrase this statement, changing it to one which conveys a truer impression of the authors' ideas. The objectionable phrase is the last half of the proposition: "that the occurrence of aggression always presupposes the existence of frustration and, contrariwise, that the existence of frustration always leads to some form of aggression."

The first half of this statement, the assertion that the occurrence

SOURCE: Neal E. Miller (with the collaboration of Robert R. Sears, O. H. Mowrer, Leonard W. Doob, and John Dollard), "The Frustration-Aggression Hypothesis," *The Psychological Review*, 1941, 48, 337–342. Reprinted by permission of the American Psychological Association and Neal E. Miller.

of aggression always presupposes frustration, is in our opinion defensible and useful as a first approximation, or working hypothesis. The second half of the statement, namely, the assertion "that the existence of frustration always leads to some form of aggression" is unfortunate from two points of view. In the first place it suggests, though it by no means logically demands, that frustration has no consequences other than aggression. This suggestion seems to have been strong enough to override statements appearing later in the text which specifically rule out any such implication (Dollard *et al.*, 1939, pp. 8–9, 19, 58, 101–102). A second objection to the assertion in question is that it fails to distinguish between instigation to aggression and the actual occurrence of aggression. Thus it omits the possibility that other responses may be dominant and inhibit the occurrence of acts of aggression. In this respect it is *inconsistent* with later portions of the exposition which make a distinction between the instigation to a response and the actual presence of that response and state that punishment can inhibit the occurrence of acts of aggression (Dollard *et al.*, 1939, pp. 27, 32–38, 39–50, 75–87, 111, 166).[1]

Both of these unfortunate aspects of the former statement may be avoided by the following rephrasing: Frustration produces instigations to a number of different types of response, one of which is an instigation to some form of aggression.

This rephrasing of the hypothesis states the assumption that was actually used throughout the main body of the text. Instigation to aggression may occupy any one of a number of positions in the hierarchy of instigations aroused by a specific situation which is frustrating. If the instigation to aggression is the strongest member of this hierarchy, then acts of aggression will be the first response to occur. If the instigations to other responses incompatible with aggression are stronger than the instigation to aggression, then these other responses will occur at first and prevent, at least temporarily, the occurrence of acts of aggression. This opens up two further possibilities. If these other responses lead to a reduction in the instigation to the originally frustrated response, then the strength of the instigation to aggression is also reduced so that acts of aggression

[1] In this later exposition a distinction is made not only between instigation to aggression and acts of aggression but also between conspicuous acts of overt aggression and inconspicuous acts of non-overt aggression. It is assumed that the former are more apt to be culturally inhibited by strong punishments than the latter.

may not occur at all in the situation in question. If, on the other hand, the first responses do not lead to a reduction in the original instigation, then the instigations to them will tend to become weakened through extinction so that the next most dominant responses, which may or may not be aggression, will tend to occur. From this analysis it follows that the more successive responses of non-aggression are extinguished by continued frustration, the greater is the probability that the instigation to aggression eventually will become dominant so that some response of aggression actually will occur. Whether or not the successive extinction of responses of non-aggression must inevitably lead to the dominance of the instigation to aggression depends, as was clearly stated in later pages of the book, upon quantitative assumptions beyond the scope of our present knowledge (Dollard *et al.*, 1939, p. 40).[2]

Frustration produces instigation to aggression but this is not the only type of instigation that it may produce. Responses incompatible with aggression may, if sufficiently instigated, prevent the actual occurrence of acts of aggression. In our society punishment of acts of aggression is a frequent source of instigation to acts incompatible with aggression.

When the occurrence of acts of aggression is prevented by more strongly instigated incompatible responses, how is the existence of instigation to aggression to be determined? If only the more direct and overt acts of aggression have been inhibited, as is apt to be the case because such acts are the most likely to be punished, then the instigation to aggression may be detected by observing either indirect or less overt acts of aggression. If even such acts of aggression are inhibited, then a different procedure must be employed. Two such procedures are at least theoretically possible. One is to reduce the competing instigations, such as fear of punishment, and observe whether or not acts of aggression then occur. The other is to confront the subject with an additional frustration which previous experiments have demonstrated would by itself be too weak to arouse an instigation strong enough to override the competing responses inhibiting the aggression in question. If the instigation from this additional frustration now results in an act of aggression, then it must have gained its strength to do so by summating with an already present but inhibited instigation to aggression. The presence of the

[2] The notions used here are similar to those employed by Professor Hull in describing trial-and-error learning. (See Hull, 1939.)

originally inhibited instigation to aggression would be demonstrated by the effects of such summation. Thus the fact that an instigation may be inhibited does not eliminate all possibility of experimentally demonstrating its presence.

At this point two important and related qualifications of the hypothesis may be repeated for emphasis though they have already been stated in the book. It is not certain how early in the infancy of the individual the frustration-aggression hypothesis is applicable, and no assumptions are made as to whether the frustration-aggression relationship is of innate or of learned origin.

Now that an attempt has been made to clarify and to qualify the hypothesis, four of the chief lines of investigation which it suggests may be briefly considered.[3]

1. An attempt may be made to apply the hypothesis to the integration and elucidation of clinical and social data. Here the fact that certain forms of aggression are spectacularly dangerous to society and to the individual is relevant. This means that acute personality conflicts are apt to arise from the problem of handling aggression and that the problem of aggression is apt to play an important role in shaping certain great social institutions such as the in-group as an organization against the out-group.

2. An attempt may be made to formulate more exactly the laws determining the different ways in which instigation to aggression will be expressed under specified circumstances. Some of the problems in this field are suggested by the phenomena of displacement of the object of aggression, change in the form of aggression, and catharsis of aggression.

3. An attempt may be made to secure more information concerning the other consequences which frustration may produce in addition to the instigation to aggression. Such an attempt would lead into studies of rational thought and problem solution as suggested in the classical work of John Dewey, and into studies of experimental extinction, trial-and-error learning, substitute response and aggression. Work along this line of investigation may deal either with the

[3] Both of the first two of these chief lines of investigation have been developed at length in *Frustration and Aggression*. No attempt was made there to elaborate upon either the third or the fourth. Thus that first effort does not purport to be a complete systematization of all principles within a single field, but rather, an exploratory attempt to apply a strictly limited number of principles to several different fields (Dollard *et al.*, *Frustration and Aggression* [New Haven: Yale University Press, 1939] pp. 18, 26).

clinical and social significance of these other consequences of frustration or with the discovery of the laws governing them.

4. An attempt may be made to improve or to reformulate the basic frustration-aggression hypothesis itself. The determination of the laws which allow one to predict exactly under which circumstances instigation to aggression may be expected to occupy the dominant, the second, the third, or some other position in the hierarchy of instigations aroused by a frustrating situation is a most important problem of this type. Another problem is the reduction of the frustration-aggression hypothesis to more fundamental principles and the more accurate restatement of the hypothesis in terms of these more basic principles. One of the steps in this direction would be to scrutinize any exceptions to the hypothesis as now formulated. Another step would involve a careful study of the early stages of the socialization of the individual in an attempt to analyze the interlocking roles of three factors: first, innate physiological reaction patterns; second, learning mechanisms; and third, the structure of the social maze which poses the learning dilemmas and contains the rewards and punishments. An empirical and theoretical analysis along these lines might lead to a fundamental reformulation giving a closer approximation of the socially and scientifically useful truths imperfectly expressed in the present frustration-aggression hypothesis.

[3]

Frustration and Regression: [1]
An Experiment with Young Children

ROGER G. BARKER, TAMARA DEMBO, and KURT LEWIN

INTRODUCTION

In psychology the term *regression* refers to a primitivization of behavior, a "going back" to a less mature way of behaving which the individual has "outgrown." A temporary regression frequently occurs in intense emotional situations with normal adults and children, particularly if these situations are unpleasant. Extreme joy, too, may lead to certain primitive actions. Fatigue, oversatiation, and sickness often cause transient regression. A more or less permanent type of regression can be observed in certain cases of senility, in a great variety of neuroses, and in functional and organic psychoses. Regression, therefore, has to be considered a common phenomenon which is related to many situations and problems and which concerns the total behavior of the person rather fundamentally.

The relation between regression and development is of special interest and significance. Knowledge of psychological development has increased considerably during the last decade. An impressive variety of developmental processes has been revealed. However, our knowledge of the factors determining development is extremely meager. Regression can be viewed as a negative development. The experimental study of regression seems to be technically somewhat easier than that of development as it is ordinarily conceived. Therefore, the indirect way of studying the dynamics of development by studying regression may prove to be fruitful for the whole problem of development.

[1] A more detailed report of this investigation will be found in a monograph by the writers (Barker, Dembo, & Lewin, 1941).

SOURCE: Roger G. Barker, Tamara Dembo, and Kurt Lewin, "Frustration and Regression: An Experiment with Young Children," Chapter XXVI, pp. 441–458. From *Child Behavior and Development*, edited by Roger G. Barker, Jacob S. Kounin, and Herbert F. Wright. Copyright, 1943. McGraw-Hill Book Company, Inc. Used by permission.

Our first step was to describe in conceptual terms the behavior and state of the person corresponding to different developmental levels. It was our hope that, since regression involves a reversal of the direction of these changes, such conceptualization might provide some basis for hypotheses as to the conditions which should lead to regression.

Development Stages

DEGREE OF DIFFERENTIATION.   There is much evidence to indicate that during development the degree of differentiation of the person and of his behavior increases greatly. This is shown by the increasing variety in all aspects of the growing child's behavior, and the shift from generalized mass activity in the fetus and neonate . . . to highly specialized actions in the child and adult. The change of the arm and hand, for example, from a highly unitary and inflexible reaching and prehensile organ in the infant to a highly differentiated instrument capable of many complicated and specialized actions in the child and adult is a case in point. . . .

TYPE OF ORGANIZATION.   The type of organization changes as the child develops. In the fetus and infant, organization of the parts is to a great extent in the nature of simple dependence of one part upon contiguous parts. Changes in state and function result from the diffuse spreading of influences to neighboring parts. . . . With the increasing differentiation of the organism, however, a stratified or hierarchical type of organization becomes increasingly important. In this type of organization there is a series of levels of control. It is exemplified in such diverse fields as motor behavior, language, and play. In each of these the occurrence of increasing numbers of behavior possibilities—e.g., independent movements of digits, new words and parts of speech, new ideas—does not result in more chaotic behavior, as would be expected if the simple diffusion-of-influence type of organization persisted. Activities are extended to longer and longer episodes in which small units of action are guided and organized by larger intentions. The independent fingers become tools under the dominance of higher centers that can enforce upon them many kinds of organized unity, whereas with the undifferentiated hand but one form of unity is possible. The larger vocabulary does not result in more profuse babbling, but in sentences organized to express controlling ideas.

SCOPE.   The scope of the child's life space increases with age. In the present connection we are particularly interested in the lengthening of time perspective (Frank, 1939). The infant lives in the present, but behavior becomes increasingly controlled by goals and expectations that are temporally more and more remote as development proceeds.

REALITY AND PHANTASY. During development the perceived environment seems to become less subjectively colored. What is perceived becomes less directly dependent on the changing moods and needs of the individual. In other words, reality and phantasy become more clearly distinguished, yet not completely separated (Lewin, 1935; Piaget, 1929). Creative activity seems to depend upon the maintenance of a particular relation between reality and phantasy. The too realistic person who does not have the imagination to "see" possibilities of changing the existing real situation cannot be creative; on the other hand, the dreamer who phantasies with no regard for the exigencies of reality is also unproductive.

There are, of course, many other characteristics of development, but these appear to be rather fundamental, and we assume that any influences that operate to change the child in directions that are opposed to them should lead to primitive behavior, i.e., lead to regression.

Conditions for Regression

This study reports an attempt to create regression in children by frustration. It can be viewed from two angles. (a) It is an attempt to clarify the nature of regression and the conditions leading to it by testing certain theoretical assumptions about regression. (b) It can be viewed as a contribution to the study of frustration.

Theoretical considerations suggest that one of the conditions which may lead to regression is a situation in which the person is in a state of blocked tension. From the description of developmental stages it follows that a state of high tension should lead to a regression in at least three respects. (a) If the state of tension in some parts is maintained at a high level, the variety of patterns of states of the person which can be realized will be greatly diminished (Barker *et al.*, 1941, pp. 40 and 247). (b) If the tension is so great that it spreads beyond the parts immediately involved and extends to the whole organism or to large parts of it, an obliteration of the divisions between weakly differentiated parts will result. In both of these cases a condition of high tension produces a dedifferentiation of the person. This, as we have seen, is a change in a direction opposite to that occurring in development, and it should show itself in a regression of behavior (Barker *et al.*, 1941, p. 241). (c) In states of high tension the hierarchical organization is likely to be affected. The direct spreading of tension will be greater when the tension is high than when it is low; hence organization processes of the type of simple diffusion of tension will increase in importance relatively to hierarchical organizing processes. This, too, is a change opposite to developmental changes and should lead to regression (.Barker *et al.*, 1941, pp. 41 and 257).

The experiments which we are going to report are not intended primarily to give proof that in a state of high tension the action toward an obstructed goal regresses to a primitive level. They are an attempt to go one step further. If the assumption is correct that a sufficiently high tension leads to regression of the individual, this condition should reveal itself not only in action toward the inaccessible goal, but also in behavior that is not related to this goal. Presenting a frustrating situation, i.e., one in which an individual is prevented from reaching a desired goal, is one way of creating tension.

PROCEDURES

In the investigation we have studied the effects of frustration upon behavior by comparing the behavior of children in a nonfrustrating or free-play situation with their behavior in a frustrating situation. We have used as a major criterion of these effects the productivity or creativity of play behavior. We chose to use constructiveness of play as one of the main indicators of the effects of frustration for the following reasons. (a) It was assumed that the constructiveness of play would vary according to the developmental stage of the child. (b) It seemed probable that, in a free-play situation, where there is very little outside pressure, behavior would reveal with particular sensitivity the inner state of the child. (c) Constructiveness of play appeared to be closely related to many aspects of the child's life space, particularly to reality and phantasy, to scope, and to degree of differentiation.

In addition to the constructiveness of play, emotional expression has been analyzed, also.

Every child was observed on two occasions. First, the child was placed in a standardized playroom and allowed to play without restriction. On a second occasion he was placed in the same room and with the same toys. However, on this second occasion there were also in the room a number of highly attractive, *but inaccessible,* toys. The latter arrangement was provided by replacing a temporary wall of the original room with a wire-net partition through which the subject could easily see the fine toys but through which loco-motion was impossible.

The subjects in the experiment were children who attended the preschool laboratories of the Iowa State Welfare Research Station. The experiment was conducted during the academic year 1935–1936. Data concerning chronological and mental ages and I.Q.'s are given in Table 1. The Kuhlmann–Binet was used with the 10 younger subjects, the Stanford–Binet with the 20 older subjects.

TABLE 1

Chronological and Mental Age Data for Subjects

	Chronological Age, Months	Mental Age, Months	I.Q.
10 Younger Subjects:			
Range	25–40	30–44	100–141
Mean	32.3	36.9	114.8
20 Older Subjects:			
Range	42–61	49–82	110–157
Mean	51.7	64.6	125.5
Total group:			
Mean	45.2	55.4	121.9

Free-Play Situation

On the floor of the (experimental) room there were three squares of paper, each 24 by 24 ins. A set of standardized play materials was placed on each square. On one square there were the following things: a little chair on which a Teddy bear and a doll were seated, a cup, a small truck and trailer, a saucer, a teapot without a lid, an ironing board and an iron (but nothing to iron), and a telephone receiver which squeaked when shaken. On another square were placed a box of crayons and two pieces of writing paper 8½ by 11 ins. On the third square there were a small wooden motorboat, a sailboat, a celluloid duck and frog, and a fishing pole with a line and a magnet for a hook.

After entering the experimental room with the child, the experimenter approached Square 1, and picking up each toy said, "Look, here are some things to play with. Here is a Teddy bear and a doll. Here is an iron to iron with," etc. In proceeding this way the experimenter named and demonstrated every toy on all three squares. Then he said, "You can play with everything. You can do whatever you like with the toys, and I'll sit down here and do my lesson." The experimenter then sat on the chair at the table.

The child was left to play alone for a 30-min. period. During this time the experimenter, as if occupied with his own work, sat at his table in the corner and took notes on the child's behavior.

Frustration Situation

PREFRUSTRATION PERIOD.   Three parts of the frustration experiment can be distinguished in the temporal order of their occurrence: (a) the prefrustration period, (b) the frustration period, and (c) the postfrustration period. [During] the prefrustration period . . . the partition dividing the room was lifted so that the room was twice the size it had been in the free-play situation.

The squares were in their places, but all toys except the crayons and paper had been incorporated into an elaborate and attractive set of toys in the part of the room that had been behind the partition.

In one corner there was a big dollhouse (3 by 3 ft.). It was brightly decorated and large enough to admit the child. Inside there was a bed upon which the doll was lying, a chair in which the Teddy bear sat, a stove with cooking utensils, and a cupboard. The ironing board with the iron on it stood against one wall, and the telephone, this time on its base with a dial and bell, was in a corner. The house had electric lights, curtains, and a carpet.

Outside the house there was a laundry line on which the doll's clothes hung. A rubber rabbit sat near the entrance to the house, and behind it was the small truck and trailer used in the preceding experiment. Nearby there was a child's table prepared for a luncheon party. On the table there were cups, saucers, dishes, spoons, forks, knives, a small empty teapot, and a large teapot with water in it.

In the other corner of the new part of the room there was a toy lake (3 by 3 ft.) filled with real water. It contained an island with a lighthouse, a wharf, a ferryboat, small boats, fishes, ducks, and frogs. The lake had sand beaches.

In all cases the children showed great interest in the new toys and at once started to investigate them. Each child was left entirely free to explore and play as he wished. During this time, the experimenter did his "lesson."

If, after several minutes, the child had played with only a limited number of objects, the experimenter approached and demonstrated the other toys, e.g., he dialed the telephone or showed the child how to get the water from the spout of the teapot. In general, the experimenter tried to call the child's attention to every toy he had overlooked. Then he returned to his place and waited until the child had become thoroughly involved in play; this took from 5 to 15 min.

The prefrustration period was designed to develop for the child a highly desirable goal which he could later be prevented from reaching. This was a prerequisite to creating frustration.

The transition from prefrustration to frustration was made in the following way. The experimenter collected in a basket all the play materials which had been used in the free-play experiment and distributed them, as before, on the squares of paper. He then approached the child and said, "And now let's play at the other end," pointing to the "old" part of the room. The child went or was led to the other end and the experimenter lowered the wire partition and fastened it by means of a large padlock. The part of the room containing the new toys was now physically inaccessible but visible through the wire netting.

FRUSTRATION PERIOD. . . . With the lowering of the partition, the frustration period began. This part of the experiment was conducted exactly as the free-play experiment. The experimenter wrote at his table, leaving the child completely free to play or not as he desired. The child's questions were answered, but the experimenter remained aloof from the situation in as natural a manner as possible.

Thirty minutes after the lowering of the partition, the experimenter suggested that the child leave.

POSTFRUSTRATION SITUATION.   After the experimenter had made sure that the child wanted to leave, the partition was lifted. Usually the child was pleasantly surprised and, forgetting his desire to leave, joyfully hurried over to the fine toys. If the child did not return spontaneously, the experimenter suggested his doing so, and a second suggestion was never necessary. The lifting of the partition at the end of the frustration period was not done with an experimental purpose, but to satisfy the desire of the child to play with the toys and to obviate any undesirable aftereffects. The child was allowed to play with the house, lake, etc., until he was ready to leave.

RESULTS

The raw data consisted of two synchronized running accounts of the course of events, one made by an observer behind a one-way vision screen, the other by the experimenter. These separate records were combined into a single, more complete, account. This was desirable since it allowed the observers to concentrate their attention upon the different aspects of the behavior that they could best observe. An observer behind a screen necessarily misses much: the verbalizations of the child are often incomprehensible, and facial expressions and gestures lose much of their significance. However, he can observe the larger aspects of the behavior adequately. On the other hand, the very wealth of detail which the experimenter within the room is able to observe causes him sometimes to miss the sequence of activities and their larger significance.

Both the free-play situation and the frustration situation produced two general kinds of behavior: (a) occupation with accessible goals, and (b) activities in the direction of inaccessible goals. We shall call the first "free activities" and the second "barrier and escape behavior." Playing with the available toys and turning on the light are examples of free activities; trying to leave the experimental situation or attempting to reach the inaccessible toys behind the barrier are examples of barriers and escape behavior. Within each of these categories it is useful to differentiate further.

Types of Behavior

FREE ACTIVITIES.   The free activity includes play with the accessible toys and diversions with nontoy objects.

Diversions, i.e., occupation with nontoy objects, include the following: (a) *Activities with the experimenter* (other than those which are social attempts to reach the inaccessible toys or to escape from the experimental situation). This behavior takes the form of conversation with the experimenter, helping him with his "lessons," and playing with him. It has been mentioned before that every effort was made not to encourage these contacts. (b) *Activities at the window:* climbing upon the sill and looking out. (c) *"Island" behavior:* Despite our continual vigilance in excluding any but standardized objects from the room, the children were forever finding additional material—e.g., a nail or a piece of string—or selecting for special attention some indifferent object in the room, as the light-switch or a crack in the floor. Such objects not infrequently appeared to have the significance of a foreign object to the child, i.e., one not naturally connected with the rest of the situation, and as such to provide a refuge or an island of escape within the situation. (d) *Looking and wandering about.* (e) *Disturbances:* reactions to outside noises, lights failing, etc.

BARRIER AND ESCAPE BEHAVIOR.   Both attempts to gain access to the toys behind the barrier and attempts to leave the experimental situation may entail (a) actual physical approaches to the inaccessible regions, such as trying to lift or climb over the barrier or kicking the door; (b) social attempts by means of requests, pleadings, coaxing, threats, etc., to get the experimenter to raise the barrier or open the door; or (c) passive directed actions such as looking at or talking about the inaccessible toys or the outside regions.

OVERLAPPING ACTIVITIES.   A subject can be involved in more than one activity simultaneously; e.g., he may ask to have the barrier raised while swinging the fish line; in these cases we speak about "overlapping regions of activity." A type of overlapping behavior of special importance to us exists when play and nonplay activities overlap. We will call this "secondary play." Primary play, on the other hand, occurs when the subject gives the play his complete attention.

SUBSTITUTE BEHAVIOR.   Passive barrier and escape behavior frequently seemed to be in the nature of a substitute for playing with the inaccessible toys or for leaving the experimental situation. This was particularly true of conversation about the inaccessible objects. Active barrier and escape behavior also seemed sometimes to be a substitution; e.g., "fishing" through the barrier, throwing the accessible toys into the inaccessible region, playing that the accessible portion of the room was a part of the inaccessible part, etc. . . .

EMOTIONAL BEHAVIOR.   Two sorts of emotional expression occurred: (a) "pure" emotional actions, e.g., whimpering, whining, restless actions, and (b) strong "emotional component" to barrier and escape behavior, play, etc.

Topology and Dynamics of the Frustration Situation

The simplest way to approach the situation of frustration is probably to treat it as a particular case of a limited space of free movement (Lewin, 1936). The space of free movement, i.e., the totality of accessible regions, may be limited by either an "inner" or an "outer" barrier or by both. In the first case a goal region . . . , a region with positive valence, is surrounded by a barrier region . . . separating it from the individual . . . , who is otherwise free. In the second case the individual is surrounded by a barrier, the goal being outside. . . .

For most of our subjects, [the first case] seems to be an adequate representation for the early periods of the frustration situation, i.e., the subject sees himself separated from the fine toys without otherwise feeling himself to be in a prison-like situation. Later the situation usually changes to that represented by the second case; he becomes imprisoned. . . .

The barrier has for the child either the character of an "objective" physical obstacle or the character of an obstacle which is created and kept in place by the experimenter, i.e., a social barrier. Frequently it is a combination of both. This is why the action toward the inaccessible toys often takes the form of both a physical attack on the barrier and a social approach to the experimenter.

SAMPLE RECORD. A part of a record will be given to acquaint the reader with the sequence and content of the course of events occurring during the experiment. This is the type of material with which we have had to work.

Child 22 is a girl fifty-three months old. Her I.Q. is 122.

Each unit of action is numbered consecutively. At the end of each unit the length of the unit in seconds is given and the constructiveness rating of the play. (Constructiveness ratings are discussed in the section immediately following.)

FREE-PLAY SITUATION

1. S.: "Here," to E., "you make me something from this clay." [2] She takes clay to Square 1 and asks, "Where are the other things?"

[2] In a few experiments a piece of modeling clay was included on the square with the crayons and paper.

(Referring to the toys present in another experiment.) "I want you to play with me." The experimenter continues recording. Constructiveness 2; 45 sec.

2. S. throws clay onto Square 2. "This is an elephant." Then finding a small peg on the floor, "Look what I found. I'll put it at his eye." Looks at it. Makes elephant sit up. Constructiveness 6; 70 sec.

3. S. starts to draw. "I'm going to draw a picture. Do you know what I'm going to draw? That will be a house. That is where you go in." Constructiveness 7; 45 sec.

4. Someone moves in another room. S.: "Who is that?" 10 sec.

5. S. goes to Square 1, shakes phone, and examines it. Manipulates phone, pretends conversation but does not use words. ("How do . . ." are the only words that E. can distinguish.) Constructiveness 5; 30 sec.

6. S. sits down on chair and looks around. "I guess I'll sit here and iron." Repeats, then says gaily, "See me iron." Constructiveness 5; 45 sec.

FRUSTRATION SITUATION

1. S. watches E. lower the partition. She asks, "I will not play on the other side again?" E. answers, "You can play here now." S. faces the experimenter for about 15 sec. with hands behind her neck. 25 sec.

2. S. looks around. 5 sec.

3. S. goes to Square 3 and examines sailboat and fish pole. Constructiveness 2; 15 sec.

4. S. stands at Square 3 and looks at barrier. 5 sec.

5. Turning to the play material on Square 3, S. takes the fish line and dangles it about sailboat. Constructiveness 2; 20 sec.

6. S. goes to the barrier and reaches through the meshes of the screen. 5 sec.

7. S. turns around, looks at the experimenter, laughs as she does so. 15 sec.

8. S. goes to Square 3, takes the fish pole, and returns to the barrier. She asks, "When are we going to play on that side?" Experimenter does not answer. Then, in putting the fish pole through the barrier, S. says, "I guess I'll just put this clear back." She laughs

and says, "Out it comes!" taking pole out again. Constructiveness 2; 35 sec.

9. S. walks to experimenter's table. 10 sec.

10. S. goes to Square 2 and manipulates clay. Constructiveness 2; 10 sec.

11. From Square 2 she looks at the objects behind the barrier and says, "I do like the balloon," and then she asks, "Who put that house there?" E. answers, "Some of my friends." She asks again, "Who put that over there?" 35 sec.

Constructiveness of Play

From this sample, the reader will gain an impression of the richness of the play which occurred. It is possible to use such manifold material for many purposes. In the present connection, we have been most interested in phases of the play that are related to the creative aspects of the child's behavior.

Constructiveness Scale. For this purpose we have made an analysis of the play activities on the basis of their constructiveness. One can distinguish variations in the type of play on a continuum ranging from rather primitive, simple, little-structured activities to elaborate, imaginative, highly developed play. We speak in the former case of low constructiveness; in the latter, of high constructiveness. In our experiment, constructiveness was rated on a seven-point scale (2 to 8) devised to be applicable to occupations with all the toys.

To demonstrate the use of this scale, we present a few examples of various constructiveness levels with the same toy, the truck and trailer. Our remarks are not definitions of the various constructiveness levels. They are intended merely to point to some characteristics of these specific examples.

Constructiveness 2. The toys are examined superficially. Example: Sits on floor and takes truck and trailer in hand. 10 sec.

Constructiveness 3. The truck is moved to a definite place or from one place to another. Example: Phone, truck and trailer, manipulated and carried to window sill. 25 sec.

Constructiveness 4. This is a somewhat more complicated manipulation of the truck. Example: Truck and trailer backed under chair. 15 sec.

Constructiveness 5. This is definitely a more complicated and elaborated manipulation of the truck. Example: Truck and trailer unloaded, detached; pulled in circles, reattached, detached, re-attached; pulled in circles. 45 sec.

Constructiveness 6.   The truck is used as a means to haul other things. Example: Takes truck and trailer. "More things are going to be hauled." Puts cup, saucer, teapot on trailer. Talks to self. "Ride along, mister." To Square 3. 60 sec.

Constructiveness 7.   The meaning of the play is an extensive "trip" or another elaborated story in which the handling of the truck is merely a part of a larger setting. Example: "Here's a car truck, and it's going out fishing, so we have to take the trailer off. First, we have to go to the gas station. Toot! Toot! Now, he's going to the gas station. Ding, ding, ding." Gets gas. Now back for the trailer and the fish pole; child has truck and takes the motor boat. Attaches it to truck and trailer. "Hmmmm! Here he goes." Behind Square 2 to 1. "Quack! Quack! Mr. Ducky come" (places on truck and trailer). Goes to Square 3. "Here's the sailboat." 225 sec.

Constructiveness 8.   Play showing more than usual originality is placed here. Example: To Square 1. Truck and trailer reattached. "I'll bring them here." Detaches truck, has it coast down trailer as an incline, reattaches. 30 sec.

The scale was constructed in the following way: The play units were transcribed serially upon cards which were grouped according to the toy or group of toys involved. Three persons working in conference arranged the play units for each toy in order of their increasing constructiveness. No attempt at independent ranking was made. The resultant order represented the consensus of opinion of the raters after discussion, disagreement, and compromise. It became evident that, irrespective of particular theories of "constructiveness," it was possible to agree upon the relative ranking of different play with the same toys.

The play units were briefly characterized and the characterizations set down in tabular form. Each rank order was assigned a numerical weight which in the final scale ranged from 2 to 8. This original table constituted the first constructiveness scale. The items were brief characterizations of very specific kinds of behavior; general categories were omitted. A record was then scored by assigning a numerical value to each consecutive play unit in the record in accordance with the rating given in the scale and weighted for the duration of the unit by multiplying by the time. The mean constructiveness of each child's play was determined by summing these values for the whole record and dividing by the total duration of play, i.e., mean constructiveness =

$$\frac{\Sigma\,[\text{Cons.}\,(u)\,\times\,\text{Dur}\,(u)]}{\Sigma\,[\text{Dur}\,(u)]}$$

where Cons. (u) = constructiveness rating of a play unit.
         Dur (u) = duration of a play unit.
         Σ [Dur (u)] = total duration of play.

RELIABILITY.   We have two sources of evidence as to the reliability of the ratings of constructiveness. One is the correlation between the constructiveness of play in different parts of the experimental period. For this purpose we have computed the mean constructiveness of play in each consecutive third of each experimental record in free play. The product-moment correlations between the mean constructiveness of play in the various third of the period are as follows:

Third of period	Correlation
1st and 2nd	.72 ± .06
1st and 3rd	.39 ± .10
2nd and 3rd	.48 ± .10

It will be pointed out later that the psychological situation was not stable throughout the experimental sessions and that it was necessary to take into consideration the changes which occurred. The above correlations are indications not primarily of the reliability of the ratings, but of the stability of the function involved. The correlation between constructiveness in the first and second third, i.e., .72, indicates, however, even if the reduction from 1.00 results entirely from unreliability of the constructive ratings, that they have a reliability sufficient for the group comparisons here involved.

Another source of evidence of reliability of the constructiveness ratings involves the use of a method which approximates the so-called "split-half" procedure used in questionnaire studies. There the score obtained by using the odd-numbered items is correlated with that obtained when the even-numbered items are used. In the present case play units of different lengths are scattered at random throughout the records. We have taken advantage of this to secure two independent estimates of constructiveness based on different lengths of play units. First we computed the mean constructiveness of each child's play based only on play units of the following lengths in seconds: 1 to 15, 31 to 45, 61 to 90, and 121 to 180. We then determined the mean constructiveness of each child's play on the basis of play units of alternative lengths, i.e., 16 to 30, 46 to 60, 91 to 120, and 181 sec. long or more. The correlation between these two independent estimates of mean constructiveness of play is .79 ± .05. The estimated reliability of constructiveness based upon all the play units is .88.

VALIDITY. If one intends to use constructiveness of play as an indication of the developmental level of a child and as an instrument for measuring the effects of regression, it must be demonstrated that, in normal children under comparable conditions, constructiveness increases with age. In other words, constructiveness of play, as determined by the constructiveness scale, should show a high correlation with age in a free situation. On the other hand, constructiveness is a characteristic of behavior which one would expect to show considerable variation from individual to individual of the same age. This means that constructiveness would be technically best fitted for our purpose if the correlation with age were high but sufficiently below 1.00 to allow for individual differences.

The product-moment correlations between mean constructiveness of primary play in the free-play situation and mental age is .73 ± .05. With chronological age the correlation is .79 ± .05. We have also calculated these correlations, omitting the data for four subjects who showed marked dissatisfaction in free play as indicated by a great amount of escape behavior. This dissatisfaction was taken to mean that these subjects were more or less frustrated in the free-play situation. Inasmuch as it was our intention to obtain the best possible estimate of the relation with constructiveness of *non-frustrated, satisfied* play, it was necessary to eliminate the subjects who did not satisfy these requirements. When they are eliminated the correlation with both mental and chronological age is raised to .81 ± .05. The mathematical regression of mean constructiveness of play upon mental age (months) in the free-play situation is linear; b equals .06.

These correlations are important insofar as they establish the fact that constructiveness of play varies positively with age between two and one half and five years (thirty to eighty-two months mental age). Although the constructiveness scale is a first attempt and may be greatly improved technically, the degree of correlation with chronological age is not far from the value which would appear to be optimal for our purposes.

The first requisite for using constructiveness of play for studying regression seems therefore to be sufficiently met, and the constructiveness scale is valid at least in the degree to which it measures something related to changes in age levels.

Frequency of Various Activities in Free-Play and Frustration Situations

Although the same types of behavior occurred in both experimental situations, their frequency of occurrence changed greatly from free play to frustration. The amount of time occupied with different activities is shown in Table 2.

TABLE 2

Average Time in Seconds Occupied by Different Activities in Free Play and in Frustration

| Activity | Mean time | | | Difference |
	Free Play	Frustration	Difference	σ diff.
Barrier Behavior	19.50	510.50	+491.00 °	11.47
Primary Play	1144.17	569.83	−574.34	8.88
Secondary Play	33.12	128.16	+95.04	4.00
Escape Behavior	49.67	112.67	+63.00	2.68
Diversions	177.17	204.17	+27.00	†

° + indicates increase in frustration; − indicates decrease in frustration.
† Not computed.

Average Constructiveness of Play in Free Play and Frustration

. . . The mean constructiveness of the play in free play is 4.99 constructiveness points and in frustration, 3.94 points. The mean regression is 1.05 constructiveness points with a standard error of .24, i.e., the mean regression is 4.39 times its standard error. Stated in terms of mental-age equivalents, i.e., in terms of the regression of constructiveness upon mental age, the mean regression amounts to 17.3 months of mental age. Twenty-two of the subjects regressed in the constructiveness of their play, three did not change, and five increased.

Analysis of the results for primary play alone indicates that the mean regression in constructiveness, although less in amount, is statistically significant.

For the 10 younger subjects, twenty-eight to forty months of age, the regression is smaller than for the 20 older subjects, aged forty-two to sixty-one months. In the former case, the mean regression is 0.58 constructiveness points, corresponding to a regression of approximately 9.6 months mental age, and in the latter case it is 1.29 points, equivalent to 21.5 months mental age. Proportionately, the per cent of decrease in functional level (as measured by constructiveness or mental-age equivalents) seems to be quite similar in the younger and the older group.

These data establish rather definitely the fact that a frustrating situation of the kind considered here reduces, on the average, the constructiveness of play below the level upon which it normally occurs in a nonfrustrating, free-play situation. Before considering how this reduction in constructiveness is effected it may be well to stress the fact that these crude results are of significance.

The results show that frustration not only affects actions related to the inaccesible goal, such as attempts to find roundabout routes of aggression against the physical or social obstacles, but that it may affect behavior in other regions of activity as well. The main expectation of the experiment has been fulfilled. More specifically, the findings show the importance of the total situation for promoting or hindering a child's creative achievement.

Measurement of Strength of Frustration

The technical arrangements were planned to provide frustration and free play. Inevitably, these effects were not secured in all cases, inasmuch as we had control over only the immediate, experimental situation and not over the expectations, anxieties, and various attitudes which the child brought to the experiment. In some instances frustration occurred in the free-play situation and in others there was no frustration in the frustration situation. In addition, all degrees of strength of frustration occurred. Thus far in the analysis we have proceeded as if the technical arrangements had functioned as intended with all subjects. The data have been classified according to the intention of the experimenters rather than according to the realities of the situation for the subject. We turn now to the analysis of some quantitative differences in the dynamical properties of the existing psychological situations. We propose to make use of certain measures of the strength of frustration in order to refine our data further.

We have been faced here with the necessity of determining the amount of frustration in the experimental situations. When such general aspects of situations are important, one notes a tendency to handle them in terms of nonpsychological concepts, i.e., in terms of economic, social, geographic, and physical categories rather than in psychological terms. We have attempted to avoid this error and to describe and measure in psychological, behavioral terms.

In doing this we are faced with two problems: (a) to determine the strength of the frustration which is created by prohibiting the subjects from reaching the inaccessible toys; (b) to determine the extent to which this background of frustration is of importance for the play activity of the children. Obviously, these factors are not independent of each other.

The problem of how the background of a situation influences behavior in an immediate situation is a general problem of prime importance. It is particularly significant for what is frequently called the larger life situation which plays such an important role in problems of personality and development.

An attempt to solve this problem touches rather basic theoretical and methodological problems. The regions of the life space which constitute the background are not a part of the activity regions in which the individual is involved at the time. They are not over-lapping with the immediate situation in the same way as the two situations in secondary play, for example. Frequently the subject will be so fully occupied with his immediate situation that he will not be aware of the background. On the other hand, the background still influences the behavior in some way. It cannot be omitted from the life space, if one is to account for the actual behavior.

It seems possible to clear up this conceptual difficulty by con-sidering the implications of the concept of contemporaneity (Lewin, 1936). In an empirical science the concept of a field existing at a given moment actually does not refer to a section without any duration through the flow of events. Even in physics it is impossible to describe such essential properties of a situation as the velocity of a point without treating the momentary situation as a segment which has a certain duration. Here it may suffice to say that in psychology, too, the situation existing at a given moment cannot be described without referring to a certain time depth. There seems to exist in psychology a definite relation between what one might call the "size" of the situation and the minimum extent of time which has to be taken into account in describing the "momentary" situation. To describe the state of the immediate situation a shorter period can usually be taken into account if one has to describe the state of a larger situation.

These considerations open up a technical way to treat problems of background without resorting to new concepts. We merely have to realize that statements concerning overlapping situations should always be related to a situation of definite size. An individual may be involved in two overlapping activities within the immediate situation, as in secondary play (e.g., play with the truck while talking about the nursery school). However, it is possible that the immediate situation does not have the character of an overlapping situation (e.g., complete attention to truck play), while at the same time the more inclusive life situation does have this character (e.g., "games" with the experimenter overlaps with nursery school situation). It seems to be conceptually permissible and, as we shall see, technically fruitful to treat the effect of the background upon behavior as an inclusive overlapping situation, involving the immediate situation and the background. Thus, the concept of relative potency (Lewin, 1938) can be used to characterize the influence of the background and of the immediate situation on behavior.

The problem of determining the amount of frustration becomes, in terms of these concepts, one of measuring the potency of the overlapping frustrating and nonfrustrating regions. We have taken as a symptom of the potency of an overlapping region, in the case of successive rather than simultaneous actions, the relative proportion of the total time occupied by the behavior to which the situation in question is coordinated. In the present case, this means that we have assumed that the potency of the frustration region is indicated by the proportion of the total experimental period occupied by frustrated behavior (barrier and escape behavior). It should be mentioned again that the inaccessible toys are not the only source of frustration. Frustration arises also when the child is prevented from leaving the experimental room, and it occurs even in the free-play situation. However, there is some indication that much of the escape behavior in the frustration situation derives from the separation from the inaccessible toys. Whatever the source of the need to leave the room, it, in its turn, leads to frustration and must be included in the total estimate. The estimate of the potency of frustration is therefore based upon the sum of both barrier and escape behavior.

Inasmuch as we are here concerned with the *change* in potency of frustration from the free-play situation to the frustration situation, we have limited ourselves to a consideration of the *difference* in the amount of time occupied with frustrated actions in the two settings. The 10 children for whom the increment of potency of frustration from the free-play situation to the frustration situation is least, i.e., those for whom the increment in duration of frustrated behavior is less than 450 sec., are considered together as the "weak" frustration group. The 20 subjects for whom this increment is greater are dealt with together as the "strong" frustration group.

Constructiveness of Play in Strong and Weak Frustration

There is a highly significant reduction in the constructiveness of play in the frustration situation in the strong frustration group, amounting to $1.46 \pm .15$ constructiveness points for primary and secondary play and $1.11 \pm .15$ constructiveness points for primary play. The first is equivalent to a regression of twenty-four months' mental age, the latter to a regression of nineteen months' mental age. With the weak frustration group, on the other hand, there is a small and not significant reduction in constructiveness, mounting to 0.23 constructiveness points for primary and secondary play and 0.12 points for primary play. When we consider both primary and secondary play, every child of the strong frustration group shows a decrease in average constructiveness during the frustration situation. The cases showing increase all fall in the weak group. When only the primary play is considered five of the seven exceptional cases fall in the weak group and only two in the strong group. These results suggest that most of the exceptions are due to differences in the dynamics of the situation, i.e., to differences in the potency of frustration.

Any doubt that real frustration, such as occurs with the strong group, leads to a significant reduction in constructiveness is dispelled by these data. It should be kept in mind, in this connection, that the selection of the strong and weak frustration groups was made on the basis of the time spent in barrier and escape behavior, a criterion which had no direct relation to level of constructiveness. The strength of frustration and the amount of regression are measured independently. Perhaps it should be emphasized, too, that these groups were not made until after the experiments were made, the records completed, and the mean constructiveness determined. Both groups were treated in all respects the same.

When the analysis is carried further and episodes of strong and weak frustration within the experimental sessions are treated separately, the magnitude of the effects of strong and weak frustration is increased.

Emotion and Regression

Pari passu with the shift in constructiveness of play there occurs a change in emotional expression. In frustration there is a decrease in freedom of expression, i.e., in the self-revealing actions. This is revealed by a decrease in play monologue and friendly conversation with the experimenter and by the frequent occurrence of masking, or tactical, social behavior. There is a decrease in the happiness of the mood in the frustration situation; happy emotional expressions decrease in frequency and unhappy expressions increase. In frustration there is an increase in motor restlessness and hypertension as revealed by loud singing and talking, restless actions, stuttering, and thumb sucking. There is an increase in aggressiveness in frustration; hitting, kicking, breaking, and destroying all increase in frequency.

THEORETICAL CONSIDERATIONS

Theory in science has two main functions: (a) to open the way to new knowledge, and (b) to organize that which is known. The first and probably most essential function determines the fruitfulness of a theory. This function is fulfilled in the following way: the theory, which at first is stated in the form of an hypothesis, envisions unrevealed facts or relations or denies certain relations which are believed to hold; in other words, the theory predicts certain facts or relations of facts. This prediction is tested, usually through experiments. It is found to be valid or invalid. However, even if it has been found valid, the new data need not be treated in terms of the theory.

It is an essential characteristic of a fruitful empirical theory that it gives birth, as it were, to new knowledge, which is then independent of its theoretical ancestry. In an empirical science new data, although discovered by theory, are something in themselves which anyone is free to interpret theoretically in his own way or to accept as mere facts. In other words, the fruitful empirical theory is instrumental in establishing new scientific data which should be able to outlive the theory.

The main results which have been presented here have actually been predicted on the basis of a theory or group of theories. The experiment was set up to test the theoretical predictions.

Originally, our experiment was designed to test the prediction that tension in strong frustration leads to a dedifferentiation of the person and therefore to regression. This regression has been found. However, the experiments have shown that, aside from dedifferentiation, other factors may enter. In other words, there are several possibilities of explaining the observed regression in a situation such as the one studied here. We shall leave it open which factor or which constellation of factors has caused the results. Probably different factors were important for different subjects.

One of the best symptoms for the increasing differentiation of the life space (including the person and the psychological environment) during development is the increasing variety of behavior. In the frustration situation the richness and complexity of the play activity definitely decreases. This regression may be caused by dedifferentiation of the individual, in which case the spreading of tension is probably important. It can be shown that the degree of differentiation of a whole is inversely related to the strength of the pressure of tension when this pressure passes certain limits that are determined by the strength of the boundaries of the natural parts of the whole. Constructiveness in play decreases with the strength of the frustration because frustration causes tension.

A decrease in the variety of behavior must also occur if a part of the whole is kept in a fixed state. This follows from certain properties of a dynamic whole. The amount of decrease depends upon the extent of the fixed areas, their degree of centrality, and their divergency from the normal level. Frustration involving a particular goal keeps a certain part of the person in a state of more or less permanent tension, and the variety of all behavior should therefore decrease.

Change in organization can be derived from the overlapping between play and barrier behavior. To be governed by two strong goals is equivalent to the existence of two conflicting controlling heads within the organism. This should lead to a decrease in degree of hierarchical organization. Also, a certain disorganization should result from the fact that the cognitive-motor system loses to some degree its character of a good medium because of these conflicting heads. It ceases to be in a state of near equilibrium; the forces under the control of one head have to counteract the forces of the other before they are effective.

The extension of the life space, particularly in the psychological time dimension, is one of the essential characteristics of development. Planning presupposes time perspective. In the frustration experiment, the experimenter interrupted the elaborate play with the beautiful toys and caused the child to move to the other side of the partition. In the previous free-play situation the child had not been interrupted and may have become confident that his play would not be interrupted. With this security he was able to make relatively long-range plans. The interference at the end of the pre-frustration period may have shattered the security and stability of the play situation. If the possibility existed that a superior power, such as the experimenter, might interfere at any moment, it might not seem worth while to develop a long-range plan. This should lead to a weakening of the connection between the reality and phantasy levels and to a narrowing of the life space with respect to its extension into the psychological future. It is possible to attribute regression in the frustration situation at least partly to this lack of security.

[4]
The Integrative Value of Concepts in Frustration Theory [1]
NORMAN R. F. MAIER and PAUL ELLEN

In two previous articles (Maier, 1956; Maier & Ellen, 1951), the evidence on which Maier's (1949) theory of frustration was built has been critically examined in the light of alternative interpretations of the data. In both instances the evaluation of the literature revealed that the crucial aspects of the experimental data had not

[1] The authors are indebted to Daniel R. Miller and L. Richard Hoffman of the University of Michigan for helpful suggestions.

SOURCE: Norman R. F. Maier and Paul Ellen, "The Integrative Value of Concepts in Frustration Theory," *Journal of Consulting Psychology*, 1956, 23, 195–206. Reprinted by permission of the American Psychological Association and Norman R. F. Maier.

been satisfactorily met by other theorists. Thus one might conclude that this theory of frustration best integrates the data on which it is based, but the question of whether it does justice to other observations and experimental findings still remains.

According to this theory, an organism's behavior potentials can be described as its repertoire of behavior, which, in line with most theories, is determined by heredity, growth conditions, and experience. The expressed or observed behavior, however, is a function of both the behavior repertoire and selective processes or mechanisms. The unique aspect of Maier's theory is the postulation of two selective processes; one operating under conditions of motivation, the other under conditions of frustration. These two mechanisms are basically different, the former selecting behavior according to the ways in which it is perceived to achieve incentives that satisfy needs; the latter, according to other principles as yet incompletely explored but different in kind from those operating under conditions of motivation. If the motivation process is operating during problem-solving performance, then frustrated behavior not only makes problem solving incidental to the needed goal object, but may actually be in conflict with it. Thus it lacks goal-orientation and therefore represents a class of behavior without a goal. Such behavior is determined largely by conditions inside the organism, so that the expression of emotions and feelings, rather than what they achieve, characteristically accompany behavior selected under conditions of frustration. The environmental condition of availability rather than need-satisfying property appears to become dominant during frustration. If behavior instigated by frustration is adaptive, at times, this is due to natural selection rather than to the organism's ability to solve a problem. Thus an angry person may strike a man who blocks his path and the man may collapse. However, if the cause of the blow is anger rather than the removal of the obstacle, the success is incidental to the purpose.

Behavior expressed under conditions of frustration is characterized by some combination of aggression, regression, and fixation (compulsion); in contrast to behavior expressed under conditions of motivation which is characterized by variability, constructiveness (maturity), and the exercise of freedom of choice. A problem situation or obstacle in the path, therefore, may either motivate an organism to show problem-solving behavior or frustrate him to show destructive, rigid, or immature behavior. The outlook in one instance is "what to do," in the other it is blaming, hostility, or self-pity. Which of these types of behavior is expressed depends upon the condition of the organism, since the same objective problem may cause both types of behavior to appear in a group of individuals.

The definitions of problem situations and of frustrating conditions are basically alike; the difference is in the behavior observed. This does not mean that some situations may not be more likely to frustrate people than others; rather, a crucial condition—an obstacle in the path of a goal—is a common characteristic of both. A determining difference in such situations is the amount of pressure or force exerted in requiring that the obstacle be circumvented. This pressure may serve either to motivate or to frustrate, and therefore produce opposite effects.

Although some individuals are more prone to show frustrated behavior than others, organisms are alike in that each possesses two qualitatively different behavior possibilities. This means that operational definitions of frustration and problem situations are essentially incomplete since the organism in question determines what effect obstacles and pressure will have on it. It follows, therefore, that even though situations may differ in degree, the organism's behavior will differ in kind.

The three concepts that characterize frustration theory, and therefore serve as critical areas for testing it, are (a) the assumption of a frustration threshold; (b) the postulation of a qualitative distinction between behaviors instigated by frustration and by motivation; and (c) the adoption of the principle of availability to account for the selection of responses that are expressed during frustration (as contrasted with the function of needs or excitatory values in motivated behavior).

These three concepts were developed in order to account for research findings obtained from the study of rats in a specific type of conflict situation. If they serve to interpret human behavior under stress, as well as animal behavior in widely different situations, there will be reason for assuming that these assumptions are fundamental principles.

Although psychoanalytic theory and frustration theory may make some of the same predictions, it is clear that the reasons supplied and the principles used will be different in origin and in kind. It is recognized therefore that in some instances two or more theories may make similar predictions and will have to be evaluated by additional criteria. With respect to the appearance of qualitative distinctions, psychoanalytic theory and frustration theory have some common features and some differences. For example, frustration theory may predict a bimodal distribution of results, while psychoanalytic theory may assume qualitative differences (discontinuous distributions) because the concept of levels or steps is inherent in the theory. For example, a child's relations with his mother may show qualitative changes as he moves from one psychosexual stage to another. However, the concept of levels does not limit the findings to bimodal distributions in behavior data, and this difference can lead to critical tests. Another difference is that frustration theory predicts behavior differences due to two physiological mechanisms, whereas psychoanalytic theory stresses cultural (learned) factors as causes of the differences. Finally, psychoanalytic theory would make one cautious in applying the theory to subhuman forms, whereas frustration theory has its origin in the study of animals below man and stresses a biological approach. If frustration-instigated behavior has survival value it is due more to natural selection than to problem-solving or decision-making.

It is not our attempt to determine whether one theory has more universality than another or whether frustration theory is the only one that can explain certain phenomena. Rather it is hoped that the universality of its basic assumptions will be better appreciated if the theory is seen in relationship to a larger variety of data and behavior settings. Since the analysis of data, in part, depends upon the theory that is tested it is hoped that other researchers will see fit to test their findings in relation to frustration theory. At the present time the failure to test for bimodal distributions in data makes it impossible in many instances to evaluate frustration theory, and this oversight may lead to the loss of critical information.

THE FRUSTRATION THRESHOLD

Frustration theory postulates that behavior that is constructive, motivated, problem-solving, or goal-oriented in nature may suddenly be replaced by behavior that is hostile (aggression), immature (regression), stubborn (fixation), apathetic (resignation), or some combination of these symptoms whenever the frustration threshold of the individual is exceeded. It is also assumed that individuals will show either constructive or nonconstructive type of behavior in a stressful situation, depending on the height of their frustration thresholds.

An experiment critical of these assumptions would be one in which the introduction of something moderately threatening or stressful caused all of the members of a group to behave in the same direction. According to frustration theory, stress (punishment) can serve as a negative incentive or as a frustrating agent, depending on whether the frustration threshold of the individual has been passed. As a consequence, punishment for aggression should cause some children to show an increase in aggressive behavior, while others should become less aggressive. Furthermore, an increase in punishment should increase the amount of group aggression, primarily by increasing the number of persons whose frustration thresholds are exceeded.

There are a variety of ways in which frustration may be induced, but these do not influence the basic character of frustrated behavior. Punishment and difficult problem situations are the most commonly used experimental methods for introducing stress. The experience of failure looms in importance as one attempts to reconcile findings.

A brief examination of the literature indicates the applicability of the concept of a frustration threshold. Allport, Bruner, and Jandorf (1949) have pointed out quite conclusively that stress and/or frustration does not cause all of the members of a group to react in the same way. Analyzing the data from life histories of 90 Jews exposed to the terror of Nazism, these authors were able to identify quite distinct behavioral reactions to the stress of National Socialism in Jews in Germany. Among the reactions manifested were resignation and defeatism, regression and fantasy reactions, conformity to the new regime, aggression and displaced aggression, and planning behavior and activities aimed at coping with the threat of Nazism by getting out of Germany. Clearly here, the stress of Nazism caused behaviors in some Jews that might be considered maladjustive (resignation, regression, displaced aggression) and in others, behaviors which can be classified as constructive. The authors point out that the simple frustration-aggression hypothesis of the Yale group (Dollard, Doob, Miller, Mowrer, & Sears, 1939) is quite inadequate to account for the wide range of behaviors exhibited under stress. The variations in behavior manifested and the possibility of grouping certain behaviors as constructive and others as nonconstructive or destructive points to the need for the postulation of a threshold principle to occount for apparently contradictory results.

The research of Barker, Dembo, and Lewin (1941) dealing with the effects of frustration on play behavior also reveals opposite reactions to interferences with need satisfaction. Out of 30 children, 5 showed an increase in constructiveness, whereas 25 showed a decrease in the constructiveness of the play behavior when the barrier was lowered separating the child from the highly valued toys. All of the 5 children showing an increase in constructiveness were in the group defined as the weak frustration group (those which showed relatively little time in performing frustration-instigated behavior, such as aggression against the barriers, and so on). Again, it is apparent from these data that introducing stress into a situation does not cause the same kind of behavior in all members of a group. . . .

THE QUALITATIVE DISTINCTION

The assumption of a threshold concept to account for the changes in behavior that occur during frustration implies that the process underlying behavior expressed during frustration is qualitatively different from the process underlying problem-solving or goal-oriented behavior, since different behavior mechanisms would be put into operation. Thus in frustration theory it is assumed that frustration-instigated behaviors differ from goal-oriented behaviors in terms of the way in which they are related to the stimulus and behavior sequences. If two behavior mechanisms exist, behavior data should be clearly divisible into two types. The classifications *goal-oriented* and *frustration-instigated* reflect the way Maier (1949) originally divided behavior in a problem situation. Accordingly, goal-oriented behavior was described as a *means* to an *end* (goal) and which is terminated when the end is reached or the need is satisfied. Frustration-instigated behavior was described as an end to a sequence and which terminates itself when full expression is possible and further aggravation to reinstate the sequence is not supplied. Because it terminates a unit of behavior the latter type is more closely linked to the situation in which the organism finds itself than is goal-oriented behavior. According to frustration theory, the search for reinforcement, need-reducing state of affairs or purpose in frustration-instigated behavior is an unrewarding task. In fact, this mental set may lead to the postulation of need systems, which often are anthropomorphic and not subject to direct empirical verification. . . .

. . . The postulation of the qualitative distinction between frustration-instigated behavior and motivated behavior, together with the concept of a frustration threshold also makes it possible to put some order into the theoretical difficulties created by the data obtained from avoidance conditioning experiments. According to frustration theory, a noxious stimulus acts as a negative incentive unless or until it is of such duration or intensity that it crosses the frustration threshold of the subject. The learning and extinction of avoidance and approach responses should obey the same laws, just so long as frustration does not enter the picture. However, if our assumptions are correct, frustration is more likely to complicate the picture when avoidance behavior is investigated. This prediction does not follow from motivation and learning theories.

In the case of the extinction of avoidance behavior, the data of Solomon and Wynne (1954) are of interest. They report that after only 3 or 4 shocks which were just subtetanizing and with a 10-sec. CS-UCS interval, the instrumental avoidance response of jumping a barrier became more and more stereotyped and the latency of the response became shorter (levelling off at 1.6 sec.). Dogs typically continued to respond to the CS for several hundred trials without showing any signs of extinction. Additional data by Solomon, Kamin, & Wynne (1953), however, show that under certain conditions extinction of these responses can occur, although the extinction was not complete in that some of the animals still failed to extinguish. Thus, when a combined procedure of preventing the response by placing a glass barrier in front of the hurdle and punishing the response was used, 14 out of 16 animals were able to extinguish their conditioned avoidance responses. Certain additional features of the experiment remain to be pointed out. First, all these animals had an intervening extinction procedure before the combined glass barrier and punishment extinction procedure was used. In 6 of the animals, a glass barrier extinction procedure alone was used for 10 days before the combined extinction procedure was instituted. When the data are analyzed in terms of this procedural breakdown, it was found that all 6 of the animals which received the glass barrier procedure prior to the combined extinction procedure extinguished their avoidance responses, whereas only 8 out of 10 of the animals which received the punishment procedure extinguished. Furthermore, the mean number of punishment shocks in the combined extinction procedure reflected the influence of whether the prior extinction procedure was the glass barrier or the punishment. That is, the six dogs that had the glass barrier prior to the combined procedure required only 8.2 shocks in the combined procedure, while the animals that had the punishment procedure required an average of 14.3 shocks, a difference which is significant at the .01 level. The important facts of this investigation that require explanation are (a) the failure of ordinary extinction procedures (omission of the UCS) to cause extinction, (b) the differences in extinction between animals receiving the glass barrier treatment and animals receiving a punishment extinction procedure prior to the combined procedure, and, finally, (c) the failure of extinction in some cases even under the best of the extinction procedures. Solomon and Wynne's principle of the conservation of anxiety seems adequate to account for the first fact—the failure of extinction to occur when merely the UCS is omitted. In other words, the short-latency avoidance reactions prevent the CS from arousing anxiety reactions, thereby conserving conditioned anxiety reactions from extinction. Also it can handle instances in which extinction occurs when only the glass barrier extinction procedure is used. However, the principle does not account for the fact that some animals never extinguish even under the best of extinction procedures. This fact of the bimodality—the split in the population—is directly explained by frustration theory because it postulates the existence of a frustration threshold. Thus animals that become frustrated by the UCS will never extinguish in the usual way, whereas those with thresholds sufficiently high to resist the frustrating effects of the UCS will be able to extinguish under certain experimental conditions. Furthermore, the difference in the proportion of animals extinguishing among those exposed to the glass barrier procedure and those exposed to the punishment procedure prior to the combined procedure also can be readily explained in terms of the dual effects of punishment postulated by frustration theory. Thus the animals exposed to the punishment procedure prior to the combined procedure received more punishment for the avoidance response than did animals exposed to the prior glass barrier procedure. According to frustration theory, this additional punishment served to make the former group rigid (i.e., resistant to extinction), because a greater number of the animals had their frustration threshold exceeded. The increased resistance manifested itself both in the number of shocks required in the combined procedure and in the smaller number of animals extinguishing.

Frustration theory does not require that all rigid behavior have its basis in frustration. Rather, this condition is but one of several under which the behavior of an organism may exhibit persistence. Other conditions are overlearning, the operation of special needs, perceptual differences, and low intelligence. Thus the failure of extinction in avoidance behavior may either reflect the operation of a frustrated condition, and thus be an instance of abnormal fixation, or simply result from the lack of a perception of more adaptive alternatives, due to the nature of the particular experimental situation. A learning-motivation concept, such as the conservation of anxiety, readily accounts for the latter alternative but is inadequate to account for the first.

The dual operation of noxious stimuli (either as a negative incentive or as a frustrating agent) should also be reflected in other types of learning experiments that utilize them as training aids. If parameters such as intensity of noxious stimulus or the number of reinforced repetitions are used, learning and motivation principles would predict a whole spectrum of response strengths when a random population is tested. However, frustration theory would predict a bimodal distribution of response strengths; fixated and nonfixated. For example, if shock were used as a driving stimulus, it would be predicted that the percentages of animals falling into the fixated group within a given level of shock intensity would increase as the shock intensity increased, but the strength of the fixation would not change. If such an experiment yielded several groupings of response strengths that were a function of the intensity of the noxious stimulus, a case could be made against the necessity for postulating a frustration threshold and the qualitative difference between fixated behavior and ordinary habits.

The part played by needs in determining response strength might be tested by using different kinds of noxious stimuli. If the results yielded as many groupings of extinction scores as types of noxious stimuli used, then a strong case could be made for the viewpoint that response strength is a function of the type of motivation used and that differences in types of motivation can cause splits in a population. Frustration theory, however, would demand bimodal distributions within each type of noxious stimulus. . . .

. . . Behaviors that are similar on the surface but that have different origins also may be expected to show basic differences when further analyzed. For example, crimes may be committed because they are perceived as the solution to a problem for the individual or because they reflect a hateful or antisocial condition. It is possible, therefore, to consider some crimes as either motivational or the product of frustration. If this is the case, cure and prevention would differ depending on the type of origin. It is also possible that these two processes may supplement each other since the behavior they elicit is not necessarily in conflict.

A paper by Jenkins (1955) describing two qualitatively different types of delinquency supports this analysis. In his treatment he differentiates delinquency as an adaptation from delinquency as a maladaptation. In the former instance, delinquent behavior differs from normal behavior only in its illegality. Its motivational aspects (acquisition, planning, integrated action, etc.) are the very ones which our culture sanctions and which keep our competitive economic system functioning. However, the delinquent behavior which he categorizes as maladaptive is "an explosion of blind destructiveness in which the individual utterly loses control of himself." [2] It represents a renunciation of goals rather than the selection and pursuit of a goal. . . .

. . . Observations of cases of problem readers likewise support this approach. It is well known that therapy helps some problem readers more than drill in reading, whereas for other children the reverse is true. Research is needed to test and evaluate these observations. If frustration theory is to serve as a guide it follows that mentally retarded children need motivation and drill; whereas frustrated children need therapy to get rid of their frustrations, including the resultant regression.

THE PRINCIPLE OF AVAILABILITY

Frustration theory postulates that when an organism is in a state of frustration, the mechanism for selecting or determining behavior differs from the one that operates during conditions of motivation.

[2] R. L. Jenkins, "Adaptive and Maladaptive Delinquency," *Nervous Child*, 1955, 11, 10.

The theory states that the specific character of the response elicited will be determined by its degree of availability to the subject and that the response will have the property of aggression, regression, fixation-rigidity, or some combination of these.

Although the mechanisms for response selection under conditions of motivation vary somewhat with the point of view of the theorist, the factors usually mentioned include excitatory value of stimulus, the needs of the individual, the previous training of the individual, and certain perceptual factors. Although availability may be implied in some of these instances it is not usually regarded as a determining influence largely imposed by the environment. Rather, response selection under motivation is consistent with the psychology of choice behavior, which in turn gives the organism a determining role in its own behavior. Behavior elicited during frustration, in contrast, takes on a character of compulsiveness so that the organism may behave in a manner that is inconsistent with its choice.

Factors which make one response more available than another require further investigations to clarify the limitations. However, enough is known to include conditions such as physical nearness, biological ease (including the response in progress), natural or unlearned preferences, primitiveness or simplicity of response, previous experience or training, and cultural or sociological influences.

Although these factors are basically different, they have one thing in common: they make certain responses more accessible to the organism than others. However, the fact that there is a multitude of determinants makes complete prediction difficult. One can test them only by equalizing the other determinants while testing one. Whether it will eventually be possible to assign weightings to the factors so as to increase prediction remains a question. It·is likely that individual differences will exist and that the weightings will fail to generalize completely.

Physical Nearness

According to this principle, things or persons near to the frustrated individual will tend to be involved in the behavior to a greater degree than other objects. Thus a frustrated person is likely to vent his hostilities on a person physically close to him. Likewise the frustrated person is inclined to use objects that are handiest for attack, rather than most efficient. For example, a woman may throw a plate while drying dishes but will strike out with a broom while sweeping.

This factor is consistent with the observations that a frustrated individual often attacks innocent bystanders, which is a puzzle from the viewpoint of problem solving. It also explains why the source of frustration sometimes is attacked since, in many instances, the object of frustration is near to the person who is frustrated. Banging on locked doors during fires or while imprisoned, even to the point of causing self-injury, is not uncommon. . . .

Biological Ease and the Response in Progress

Other things being equal, the response selected under frustration is likely to be one that is convenient for the individual because of his make-up or particular environmental circumstances at the time of frustration. Pushing is easier than pulling, and kicking is easier under some conditions than others. Thus the form of aggression may vary with individuals and with circumstances. Response fixation may also be influenced by ease or convenience. A forward movement is easier than a turn, and continuation of a response is easier than a change. For this reason, the response in progress at the time of frustration tends to be highly accessible, unless the conditions of frustration block it in some way.

An experimental demonstration of this factor was made by Kleemeier (1942). He trained some rats to go right, others left, and still others to go straight ahead at a junction in a maze. Mastery of one of these responses was their first habit. He then tried to develop a second habit by punishing the rats with electric shock for following the first habit. It was found that punishment fixated responses but that other factors determined which response became fixated. Usually either the old response (the one in progress) persisted or a response to the alley lying straight ahead (the one most accessible) was fixated. When the forward alley was the initial response, it was seldom abandoned. This experiment nicely demonstrates how the physical arrangement of a situation and the response in progress makes certain behaviors psychologically more accessible to the subjects. . . .

Unlearned Preferences

Personal or species preferences, even when unlearned, constitute another factor related to availability. Animals may have preferences for brightness, color, position, etc., when presented with discrimination choices, and it may be assumed that such preferences will influence the response selected during frustration. . . .

Simplicity of Response

A simple response is more likely to become fixated, other things being equal, than a complex or involved one. In the Michigan experiments (Maier, 1949), it was the consistent finding that rats fixated position responses more often than discrimination responses. Acccording to this factor it follows that an act of aggression is more likely to be a gross or primitive type of movement than a fine skill. As a corollary to this hypothesis it would be expected that complex activities should be more susceptible to stress variables than simple activities; and they should reflect this increased susceptibility both in terms of differences in rates of acquisition and in a more rapid deterioration under stress. . . .

Training

Kleemeier (1942) found that a frustrated rat will fixate a previously learned alley in preference to a new one if other things are equal. However, this tendency is not as strong as is usually supposed, and is offset by the greater importance of the response in progress and the ease of movement. Nevertheless, it must be included as a factor making for response availability during frustration. According to this principle, a trained boxer is more likely to hit with a skilled jab than with a haymaker when engaged in a barroom brawl, while a wrestler in the same situation would be more inclined to select a haymaker.

This factor perhaps would not be crucial for testing frustration theory because learning is regarded as an important selector of behavior in most theories. Frustration theory makes learning a less important factor, however, and in this respect it might become an issue for a critical experiment.

Sociological and Cultural Influences

Although cultural influences are learned, the effect of culture is somewhat more complex than that of learning. One important complication is that social pressure operates to train and to motivate a social individual to follow the behavior pattern of his group. Although research in this important area is sketchy and inconclusive it should be explored because of its potential theoretical importance.

According to this factor various cultural groups should express their frustrations differently. When frustration occurs, males should be more likely to show aggression than females in certain cultures but not in others—depending upon the special values of the culture. It also follows that the proportion of physical fighting to verbal attacks in playgrounds should vary in different social groups, being greatest in groups where a given form of aggression is most acceptable. The objects selected for attack as well as the mode of attack likewise will be influenced by cultural factors. Thus scapegoats for attack may be Negroes, Mexicans, Japanese, Irish, Jews, etc., depending on locality or cultural group in which the frustration occurs. This cultural influence would supplement the factor of nearness. . . .

Sex, Body Structure, and Personality

Sex differences and variations in body build also may be expected to influence the availability of responses. It is well known that an unhappy home life causes boys and girls to express their frustrations differently. Although part of these differences may be due to training or cultural influences, it is best to keep this category separate from others until such related factors are found to be fully overlapping.

, One relevant experiment related to this factor is that of Marquart (1948). She observed men to be more likely to show hostility (aggression) in her frustration experiments than women, while women were more inclined to cry (regression) than men. . . .

SUMMARY

The present paper has dealt with the three major explanatory concepts of frustration theory: the frustration threshold, the qualitative distinction between frustration-instigated behavior and motivated behavior, and the principle of availability. Illustrative data from the literature of various research areas were analyzed from the point of view of the theory to demonstrate how its concepts could be utilized in explaining and integrating these diverse kinds of data. In addition, an attempt was made to determine whether these concepts could clarify research areas that were confused by contradictory data. This was done by attempting to integrate the contradictory data within the framework of the theory and also by suggesting questions that might be subject to empirical verification.

The factors that determine the form of expression that frustration will take and the types of behavior pathology that may appear were examined. It is clear that the nature of the provoking conditions, the types of needs that are denied, and the intensity of need deprivation are insufficient variables to account for the findings. Research in this area is badly needed and it is hoped that the issues raised will suggest additional problems to explore and new categories of data to tabulate.

Although the present elaboration of the concepts of frustration theory led to an explanation and integration of material from a variety of sources, there is no intent to convey the impression that frustration theory is a completed system. Many details and relations need to be extended and clarified. Since one of the requirements of a meaningful behavior theory is that it be helpful in generating testable hypotheses and concepts, it is hoped that in pointing up crucial issues in a wide range of data, differences in theoretical positions can be subjected to experimental investigation and hence to a further elaboration of the theory. A prematurely closed theory may be a handicap to new research because it delimits the regions explored. What is needed is the location of new areas.

[5]

Frustration and the Quality of Performance: II. A Theoretical Statement

IRVIN L. CHILD and IAN K. WATERHOUSE

What is the effect of frustration on the quality of performance? There appears to be a dual tradition in the writings of psychologists and others who have given attention to this problem.

SOURCE: Irvin L. Child and Ian K. Waterhouse, "Frustration and the Quality of Performance: II. A Theorteical Statement," *Psychological Review*, 1953, 60, 127–139. Reprinted by permission of the American Psychological Association and Irvin L. Child.

First, there is a tradition that frustration leads to improved quality of performance. Dewey's often cited account of why thinking occurs stresses the role of a problem or difficulty as the occasion for creative intellectual activity (Dewey, 1910). Difficulty in such a situation often is an instance of frustration.[1] In more general accounts of the psychology of adjustment, unreduced tension is shown as giving rise to various forms of adjustment, of which some may be of high intellectual quality (Shaffer, 1936). On the level of society as a whole there are notions—such as Toynbee's (Toynbee, 1947)—that the protracted existence of a challenge, often in the form of difficulty in meeting the needs of bare subsistence, is the condition for the joint constructive activity that produces a new civilization.

Second, there is also a tradition that frustration leads to lowered quality of performance. This is perhaps the more apparent part of the thesis of psychoanalysis and psychology of adjustment, since, on the whole, adjustments of poor quality to frustration have received the greater attention from therapists. This tradition is also evident in much of the discussion about the disorganizing effects of emotion [as reviewed, e.g., by Leeper (Leeper, 1948)], inasmuch as emotion is often produced by frustration. Barker, Dembo, and Lewin's study of frustration and regression (Barker *et al.*, 1941) is often cited in simple confirmation of this tradition, to the neglect of the rest of its content. Most recently this tradition is represented in Maier's systematization of the effects of frustration (Maier, 1949), as most of the effects he deals with would doubtless be considered to be of poor intellectual quality.

There is, then, an apparent conflict of belief in this matter. Indeed, the conflict appears strikingly in some general textbooks in psychology. In a chapter on thinking and reasoning frustration is viewed as the condition for more organized behavior, and in a chapter on emotion it is viewed as the condition for less organized behavior.

---

[1] We are using *frustration* in a broad sense to refer to prevention of a person's direct progress toward a goal, not wishing to prejudge by definition the importance of various distinctions that can be made among the variety of events that fit this definition. We heartily agree with Brown and Farber's emphasis on the need to distinguish sharply between this definition of *frustration* and its definition as referring to a state of the organism (J. S. Brown and I. E. Farber, "Emotions Conceptualized as Intervening Variables—With Suggestions Toward a Theory of Frustration," *Psychological Bulletin,* 1951, 48, 480). But we feel it more useful to apply the term to the *event* of prevention of a person's progress toward his goal than to a *state* which may in some cases be inferred from the event.

The failure to use a common term such as frustration in the two chapters apparently permits the contradiction to go unnoticed.

Is this apparent contradiction due merely to failure to appreciate the role of severity of frustration, minor frustrations leading in fact to an improvement in quality of performance and major frustrations to the opposite, as might be inferred from the settings in which these contrary effects are often discussed? Presumably not in any very uniform way, else why would anyone swear when he stubbed his toe, and how could any prisoner ever carry through successfully an ingenious plan for escape?

The greatest advance toward resolving this contradiction has been made by Barker (Barker, 1938) and by Barker, Dembo, and Lewin (1941). By drawing upon their contributions, upon other aspects of psychological theory, and upon evidence obtained in a variety of pertinent studies, we hope to advance still further toward an understanding of the factors which influence the direction of change in quality of performance that results from frustration.

We have found it convenient to deal with three problems which it is useful to separate for purposes of analysis:

I. Effects of frustration in one activity upon the quality of performance in a second activity.

II. Effects of frustration in one activity upon the quality of performance in that activity.

III. Effects of frustration upon the quality of a person's behavior as a whole.[2]

The three sections of this paper will be devoted to these three problems in turn. For the sake of brevity only one of these problems—the second one—has been selected for detailed treatment.

I. Effects of Frustration in One Activity upon the Quality of Performance in a Second Activity

The well-known experiment of Barker, Dembo, and Lewin is presented by those authors as dealing with a generalized effect of frustration upon the constructiveness of a person's behavior as a whole.[3] Actually, a critical analysis of the procedures and results

[2] This section of the original paper has been omitted in this reprint because of space limitations.

[3] See Roger G. Barker, Tamara Dembo, and Kurt Lewin, "Frustration and Regression: An Experiment with Young Children," *University of Iowa Studies of Child Welfare*, 1941, 18, No. 1, 46.

indicates that it can only be said with certainty to deal with the effects of frustration in one activity upon the quality of performance in a second activity. The activity frustrated was children's play with a highly attractive set of toys; the second activity, in which quality of performance was measured, was play with a much less attractive set of toys. The theoretical discussion by Barker, Dembo, and Lewin, like their data, is most directly relevant to the problem of this section.

In discussing this problem Barker (1938) and, less sharply, Barker, Dembo, and Lewin (1941) make a definite contribution to an understanding of the factors which determine whether frustration will lead to a better or poorer quality of performance. The suggestion they make about frustration in relation to poorer quality of performance we would rephrase as follows: frustration of one activity will produce lowered quality of performance in a second activity to the extent that it leads to the making of responses which interfere with the responses of the second activity. Barker, Dembo, and Lewin minimize the role of this sort of hypothesis in explaining their results. We have shown in a previous paper (Child & Waterhouse, 1952), however, that their results actually support this hypothesis very strongly; and we feel that this is the most important empirical contribution of their study.

The opposite effect, improved quality of performance, is ascribed by Barker, Dembo, and Lewin to what we would call an increase, resulting from frustration of one activity, in the strength of drives which support the second activity. Barker (1938) suggests three conditions under which such drives are likely to be strengthened in a way which results in increased quality of performance. We would rephrase them as follows:

1. When the second activity can be and is motivated in part by the original, unreduced drive which had been motivating the frustrated activity, so that the second activity functions as a substitute for the first.

2. When frustration-produced drive leads to an attempt to escape from reminders of the frustrated activity, and preoccupation with the second activity is the mode of escape hit upon.

3. When the person was previously especially unmotivated with respect to the second activity, for it is then supposed that quality of performance may be favorably influenced by increased drive more than it is unfavorably influenced by interference.

These all seem to be significant suggestions, and in each case allied fields of research could provide evidence that indirectly supports their plausibility. They have not, however, been tested systematically in research on quality of performance, though they are drawn upon by Barker, Dembo, and Lewin in interpreting the behavior of individual subjects who in their experiment showed an increase instead of a decrease in constructiveness after frustration.[4]

This contrast between the effects of interference and of increase in relevant drive, resulting from frustration, seems to us of fundamental importance, though it leaves many questions unanswered. This same contrast will be made in connection with the second problem, to be considered in the following section of this paper. Other points to be made in the following section can also be applied, with modification, to the present problem, but we shall discuss them explicitly only with reference to the second problem. There remains to be made here, however, a special point about the interference effect of frustration upon a second activity, a point which is distinctive for the problem of this section and essential for putting into proper perspective the role of frustration here.

The point is this: Frustration of the first activity may, *in comparison with active pursuit of the first activity*, actually increase the quality of the second activity by reducing the amount of interference with it. This is particularly likely to be true if the two activities are essentially alternatives of which the first activity is the preferred or dominant one. For if in this case the preferred activity is being pursued without frustration, all the overt responses which make it up are present to interfere with possible pursuit of the second activity. If, on the other hand, the preferred activity is thoroughly frustrated, there may remain, as possible sources of interference with the second activity, only implicit tendencies to return to the preferred activity. Interference arising solely from implicit tendencies, from thoughts, seems likely on the whole to be much less severe than interference arising from successful overt pursuit of a dominant activity. We suggest that one aspect of the Barker, Dembo, and Lewin experiment can probably be viewed in this light, though the design of their experiment does not permit our suggestion to be tested. We can only illustrate our meaning by suggesting a variation of conditions which was not actually used in their experiment.

The constructiveness of children's play with relatively unattrac-

[4] See Roger G. Barker, Tamara Dembo, and Kurt Lewin, "Frustration and Regression: An Experiment with Young Children," *University of Iowa Studies of Child Welfare*, 1941, 18, No. 1, 179–186.

tive toys was initially measured in a free-play period, with no other toys in sight. Later, the constructiveness of their play with these same toys was measured during a frustration period, in which the children had just been interrupted in play with more attractive toys and these more attractive toys remained in sight behind a wire barrier.[5] The constructiveness of play with the unattractive toys was lower during the frustration period than it had been during the free-play period; but still, it was an activity of considerable constructiveness, or quality. Our contention is that the constructiveness of play with the attractive toys would not have been as high as it was had it not been for the frustration arising from inability to play with the attractive toys. For, suppose that instead of being frustrated, the children had been allowed to continue play with the more attractive toys, the unattractive toys being put off by themselves in another part of the room. What, in this case, would have been the quality of performance in the second activity, i.e., interaction with the unattractive toys? We would predict that it would fall into a very much lower level still—that it would be largely confined to glances and sporadic beginnings of play, rapidly interrupted by return to the more attractive toys.[6]

Frustration of a preferred activity, then, may produce for a second activity a degree of interference which is intermediate—intermediate between the greater interference which would have occurred in the absence of the frustration and the lesser interference which would have occurred in the total absence of the preferred activity. . . .

. . . In sum, then: Where quality of performance is lower than might be expected, and this lowering appears to be connected with the course of other activities, frustration of other activities is one possible source of interference; but successful pursuit of other activities may be a more important one. The college student who is frustrated in his attempts to arrange a date for the evening may not learn his German vocabulary that evening as well as he could; but it's a good bet that he'll learn it better than if he had had a date.

[5] For the purposes of the general point under discussion it should be noted that the play with the attractive toys is here regarded as the first activity, and the play with the unattractive toys is regarded as the second activity.

[6] This prediction, as applied to the Barker, Dembo, and Lewin experiment, is complicated by the fact that children could integrate the two sets of toys in a single play activity. For our point to be made, one must suppose that the rules of the situation did not permit this integration—a restriction which, for many situations to which one would wish to generalize, is imposed by the very nature of the activities.

II. Effects of Frustration in One Activity upon the Quality of Performance in That Activity

In dealing with the effects of frustration in one activity upon the quality of ongoing performance in that activity itself, we shall organize our discussion under five main headings. These represent five kinds of process or event which may influence the effect that frustration has on the quality of performance. This analysis has been difficult, because the several processes or events are closely interconnected and in many an instance would all be operating at once. We believe, however, that this sort of analysis is useful for reaching an understanding of the effects we are dealing with.

A. Extinction of the Initial Response to the Situation

When a person is frustrated in some activity, the situation to which he is responding is thereby somewhat changed. The extent to which it is changed, however, varies, and in some instances it may be useful, in predicting his response, to consider the situation to which he is responding as essentially the same as it was before the frustration. When this is a useful approach to make, Hull's concept of the habit-family hierarchy (Hull, 1934), expressed in a somewhat more general form, suggests the importance for our problem of the extinction of the initial response to the situation.

A person may be conceived of as having, in any specific situation, tendencies to make various response sequences which may all potentially lead to the goal toward which he is oriented. These various response sequences may be thought of as a hierarchy, the various members of which differ in habit strength (that is, in the strength of the tendency for them to be evoked). The sequence for which the habit strength is initially strongest will be the one first evoked. If the resulting activity is frustrated, its habit strength is diminished by the process termed extinction. With persisting frustration, its habit strength may be reduced below that of the other members of the hierarchy. At this point the other response sequences in the hierarchy will begin to be evoked. The effect of frustration upon the quality of performance in this case, then, will depend upon the relative quality of the initial response sequence which is extinguished and of the other response sequences which are then evoked instead.

On the whole, it seems likely that the initial response sequence will be the sequence of highest quality in the hierarchy. The reason for this expectation is that the response sequence of highest quality is likely to have been the most strongly and consistently rewarded in similar situations in the past, and thus to have become the response sequence of greatest habit strength and the one first to be evoked. . . .[7]

. . . The effect of extinction of the initially dominant response tendency is not, of course, necessarily a lowering of quality of performance. The order of response sequences in the hierarchy for the given situation may be determined by generalized effects of learning which took place in a previous situation (or situations) which was appreciably different from the present one. In particular, the previous and present situations may differ in the quality of performance which would be judged to characterize particular response sequences if evoked in those situations. Thus the present situation may first evoke a response sequence which was of high quality in former situations but of low quality in this situation; extinction of the tendency to respond with this sequence *may* in that case lead to the evocation of a response sequence lower in the hierarchy but of higher quality in this situation.

B. Situational Changes

In the preceding section we considered certain implications that follow when the frustrated person may be considered to be still responding to essentially the same situation. In this section we turn to certain implications which follow when the character of the frustrating circumstances is such that the person must be considered to be now responding to a situation very different from that which preceded the frustration. We shall not deal here with the fact of frustration itself as a new element in the situation to which the person is distinctively responding; this matter we shall discuss in Section D. We shall deal here simply with specific changes in the situation which are inherent in the specific manner by which the frustration is brought about.

The point we are concerned with here is this: One effect of frustration is to alter the person's situation in such a way that behavioral possibilities are changed, and this alteration has implications for the possible quality of the person's performance.

On the one hand, frustration may alter the situation in such a way

[7] We are indebted to Dr. Gregory A. Kimble for suggesting this point to us.

as to render impossible any responses of high quality directed at the original goal. There is an approach to this condition in the Barker, Dembo, and Lewin experiment (1941). The highly constructive behavior of complex play with the desirable toys was rendered impossible by making those toys completely unavailable to the child. If the constructiveness of behavior in relation to the goal of playing with those inaccessible toys was characteristically reduced by frustration (no systematic evidence was in fact collected on this point), was it not largely because this highly constructive behavior was made impossible and no other equally constructive behavior in relation to that goal was possible for most of the children? . . .

. . . On the other hand, frustration may alter the situation in such a way as to make possible the achievement of the goal by acts of higher intellectual quality than were previously possible or appropriate. . . . This sort of effect may be seen in the Barker, Dembo, and Lewin study if one looks solely at the means by which the child achieved, or might have achieved, contact with the desirable toys. When they were freely available to him, he simply approached and touched them. When a barrier was interposed, the only behavior that might possibly have led him to these toys was a much more complex sequence of influencing the experimenter, though, as it happened, it had been predetermined that even this should not be successful.

C. Quality of the Responses Available for Performance

In Sections A and B we have shown that the elimination of one response, as a result of frustration, may influence the quality of performance. In Section A, we considered the elimination of one response through extinction. In Section B, we considered the elimination of one response because of the removal of some kind of environmental facility or support which is essential for its performance. Just how this elimination of one response will affect the quality of performance depends, of course, both upon the quality of the eliminated response and upon the quality of the other responses which then come to be made. We must now consider explicitly, therefore, the question of what variables influence the quality of the responses available in the person's repertoire and likely to be made if frustration eliminates the initial response.

In the case we have dealt with in Section A, where the person may be considered as responding to essentially the same situation before and after frustration, we have already suggested that Hull's concept of the habit-family hierarchy provides a useful theoretical schema for dealing with this problem. The quality of the new behavior resulting from frustration would be predicted from the quality, as responses in this situation, of the responses next to the initially dominant one in the hierarchy. Actual application of this schema, of course, requires measurements both of quality and of habit strength of response sequences. Such measurements are certainly possible for complex human behavior, and have been made in connection with other problems. With reference to studies already done which are directly relevant to this problem, however, the schema can only be applied by using gross judgments of great differences in quality and habit strength between the initial response sequence and other response sequences, as in our interpretation of the experiments we cited in Section A.

In the case we have dealt with in Section B, where the situation to which the person is responding must be considered as radically changed, the same theoretical schema of Hull's may be considered as sometimes applicable. Here the quality of performance after frustration would be predicted from knowledge of the quality represented by the response sequence *highest* in the habit-family hierarchy for this new situation. . . .

. . . Regardless of how the elimination of the initial response is brought about, however, the concept of the habit-family hierarchy is not by itself adequate to deal with all cases. For in many cases the initial response sequence is replaced, not by some other response sequence which has a predictable habit strength resulting from previous reward or non-reward in similar situations, but rather by some novel response sequence which has never previously been performed by the person in any situation.

Now, under these circumstances, the problem of predicting the effect of frustration upon quality of performance becomes the specific problem of predicting whether a person, in the face of frustration, will produce novel responses and whether these novel responses will be of high or low intellectual quality. . . .

. . . First of all, there is research on intelligence as an organismic variable which influences the person's reactions in a variety of situations. If intelligence tests measure so broadly relevant a variable as is often hoped, that variable should be highly useful in predicting the quality of a person's response to frustration—in predicting, in other words, the likelihood that a frustrated person will hit upon a novel response of high quality rather than persisting in an unsuccessful response or making novel responses of poor quality.

Second, if this first point is correct, research on determinants of intelligence is also relevant to the present problem. If heredity, nursery-school training, institutionalization, intellectual character of the home environment, etc., influence general intelligence, they should influence the likelihood that the frustrated person will make a novel response of high quality.

Finally, research on factors in the immediate situation which influence the adequacy of reasoning and problem solution is relevant to the present problem. Such research has not ordinarily been formulated as dealing with frustration. When we speak of frustration, we ordinarily think of a person as at first anticipating steady progress toward his goal, and at a later point encountering a barrier. In experimental studies of reasoning and problem solution, on the other hand, the barrier is generally present at the outset; the subject is asked to orient himself toward a goal which is obviously difficult to attain. But the determinants of quality of response under these special circumstances should certainly help to illuminate also response to problem situations as they arise in the form of frustration in normal life. . . .

D. Habits of Responding to Frustration

We have so far considered the person as responding to the situation in which frustration is occurring, but not as responding to the fact of frustration per se. But the occurrence of frustration is, of course, itself a distinguishable aspect of the situation to which the person may respond distinctively. A person might conceivably have general habits of responding to all frustrations, or he might have more specific habits of responding to particular classes of frustration which for him were distinctive. The possible responses which might, in various individuals, have come to be elicited by the cue of frustration are of course innumerable. We propose to call attention here to several classes of response which appear to have a special relevance for the influence of frustration upon quality of performance.

1. PERSISTENCE VS. WITHDRAWAL. Persistence in striving for the goal, in the face of frustration, is a response which keeps the individual in the situation and makes possible the emergence of novel responses of high intellectual quality, though whether such re-

sponses do in fact emerge will then depend upon such variables as those considered in Section C. The degree of persistence appears to be in part determined by habits of response to frustration. Grosslight and Child (1947) showed, for one experimental situation, that subjects who had been subjected to frustration in the experiment and rewarded for persistence, subsequently persisted much longer in the face of continuous frustration than did subjects who had experienced only success until the time of continuous frustration.[8] In the same study tentative evidence was found that the first group of subjects, as a result of their persistence, were more likely to make novel or creative responses of a sort which under many circumstances would lead to a removal of the frustration. The second group of subjects, on the other hand, were more likely simply to withdraw from the situation or confine their responses to mere staring.

2. INTERFERING RESPONSES.   Another difference among persons in their habits of responding to frustration has to do with their tendency to make responses which interfere with effective pursuit of the original activity and thus lower its quality. Thus Waterhouse & Child (1953) used a questionnaire to measure the extent to which individuals habitually respond to frustration with potentially disruptive reactions, such as aggression, self-blame, and self-justification. They found that people scoring high on this personality measure, when subjected to experimental frustration, showed a lowered quality of performance; people scoring low on this personality measure, on the other hand, when subjected to the same experimental frustration, actually showed an improved quality of performance. . . .

3. DRIVE-PRODUCING RESPONSES.[9]   Among the responses a person

[8] A finding, of course, parallel to the typical outcome of experiments on partial reinforcement using traditional conditioning techniques (Jenkins & Stanley, 1950).

[9] Brown and Farber (1951) have recently published an article which, while not focused on the problem of quality of performance, is highly relevant at this point to our treatment of this problem. Their " 'emotional' interpretation of frustration behavior" might be regarded in large part as a much more thorough attack on the problem we deal with under the label of "drive-producing responses." We differ from them in viewing an emotional interpretation, and what they call nonemotional interpretations, which would include most of the rest of our treatment, not as alternative approaches (J. S. Brown and I. E. Farber, "Emotions Conceptualized as Intervening Variables—With Suggestions Toward a Theory of Frustration," *Psychological Bulletin*, 1951, 480) but as two aspects of theory which need to be put together for the prediction of behavior.

may make to frustration are internal responses which create or strengthen drive states. Indeed, some of these drive-producing responses are among the interfering responses we have mentioned in the preceding paragraph. Drive-producing responses, however, have two special properties in relation to the present problem.

(a) Certain drive states produced in response to frustration may operate to increase the motivation supporting the goal-oriented activity and thereby to improve the quality of performance. Individuals who have habitual tendencies to react to frustration with responses which create or strengthen these particular drive states would then improve their performance in the face of frustration. . . .

(b) Quality of performance is likely to be greatly influenced not only by the drive states created by frustration, but also indirectly by other responses which are evoked by those drive states. The individual's habits of responding to drive states—in particular to the drive states likely to be evoked by frustration—thus are crucial in determining the effect of frustration upon the quality of his performance in the original activity. Among the drive states likely to be evoked by frustration are states of intense general emotion. These emotional states provide an apt example to illustrate the point we wish to make here.

Psychology textbooks often refer to the disorganizing effects of severe emotion (Leeper, 1948). Undoubtedly severe emotion does often have a disorganizing effect and thus reduces the quality of performance in the face of frustration. In part this may be because the emotional responses themselves are to some extent incompatible with the ongoing instrumental activity. But in even greater part the disorganizing effect may have to do with responses *to* the emotional state. A typical person in our society is likely to have well-established tendencies to react to strong emotion with various responses—such as withdrawal from the emotion-arousing situation, close attention to the emotional experience, worry, expressive behavior such as swearing and gesturing—which all tend to interfere with efficient pursuit of the original goal-oriented activity. We would suspect that persons with a different habit structure might react to the same emotional states in themselves with a higher, rather than a lower, quality of performance. This appears to be the assumption underlying certain aspects of military training and implicit in the belief that seasoned troops are more dependable than inexperienced ones —the assumption that training can modify the way a person responds to an intense emotional state, indeed can modify it so radically that intense emotion may come to have an organizing rather than a disorganizing effect on behavior.

E. Situational and Task Variables in Relation to the Fact of Frustration

In Section D we have shown that the person's habits help determine whether his response to the fact of frustration will be such as to improve, or such as to detract from, the quality of his performance. In this section we wish only to point out briefly that the person's response to the fact of frustration will also be influenced by a variety of situational and task variables. The same kinds of response to frustration remain pertinent here.

Differences in instructions or in initial set given by the situation, for example, may influence the likelihood that frustration will evoke persistent striving or, on the other hand, withdrawal. Various specific circumstances in the situation may help determine whether frustration evokes responses which interfere with the original activity, and what effect it has on drive states and on responses to these. The extent to which heightened drive can lead to improved performance, and the extent to which other responses are incompatible and produce interference, may vary with the exact nature of the task or activity in which quality of performance is being judged. In all these ways, then, the kinds of responses we have considered in Section D are relevant to the effect of frustration on quality of performance, but relevant not only as a function of the person's habits but also as a function of situational and task variables. . . .

[6]

Emotions Conceptualized as Intervening Variables— With Suggestions Toward a Theory of Frustration

JUDSON S. BROWN and I. E. FARBER

The majority of contemporary psychologists would probably agree that the problems commonly associated with the concept of *emotion* must be treated in some detail by a systematic theory of behavior that aspires to even a moderate degree of comprehensiveness. Although a few attempts have been made to delete the term from the vocabulary of psychology, the concept persists in intruding itself into psychological writings, albeit often, following the current fashion, under the headings of conflict, frustration, and anxiety. In spite of the widespread belief in the importance of the phenomena subsumed under these headings and the imperative need for a clear understanding of their influence upon behavior, it is evident that no genuine order can be discerned within this field. Instead, examination of current treatments of emotions reveals a discouraging state of confusion and uncertainty. Substantial advances have been made in recent years with respect to theories of learning and motivation, but the phenomena of emotion have not, as a rule, been considered in these formulations and remain a tangle of unrelated facts. Many reasons could undoubtedly be advanced to account for the amorphous and ill-defined structure of existing theories of emotion; the phenomena are complex, manifold, evanescent, and difficult to measure. It is the opinion of the present writers, however, that the confusion surrounding this concept is primarily the result of serious misconceptions regarding the nature of theory construction in psychology and the kinds of procedures that must be followed if adequate theories of emotion are to be developed and integrated into more comprehensive systems of behavior.

SOURCE: Judson S. Brown and I. E. Farber, "Emotions Conceptualized as Intervening Variables—With Suggestions Toward a Theory of Frustration," *Psychological Bulletin*, 1951, 48, 465–495. Reprinted by permission of the American Psychological Association and Judson S. Brown.

The aims of the present paper are (1) to indicate what appear to be the essential requirements of an adequate theory of emotion (or emotions), (2) to consider the implications of these requirements for certain traditional problems of emotion, (3) to examine briefly some current treatments of emotion in the light of these requirements, and (4) to illustrate the proposed method of conceptualization by presenting the outlines of both a "nonemotional" and an "emotional" theory of behavioral phenomena commonly ascribed to anger or frustration.

I. GENERAL REQUIREMENTS OF A THEORY OF EMOTION

Since there is no unanimity of opinion with respect to what constitutes adequate theorizing in the case of, say, learning, or perception, or motivation, it is scarcely to be expected that the general requirements for a theory of emotion suggested herein will be acceptable to everyone. Without examining the problems of psychological theory construction in detail, therefore, we shall simply attempt to outline the steps to be followed in the light of what appear to be the most adequate techniques available at present. Specifically, we shall attempt to apply to emotion certain of the fundamental ideas of theory construction (Bergmann & Spence, 1941; Hull, 1943a; Hull, 1943b; Spence, 1944; Spence, 1948; Spence, 1951; Tolman, 1932; Tolman, 1936) developed in recent years in connection with more comprehensive theories of behavior.

At the outset we would insist that the initial step in developing a theory of emotion is the frank recognition that emotion, if it is to enter usefully into scientific thinking, must be regarded as an *invention* or *inference* on the part of the psychologist. Emotion is not a *thing* in the simple, naive sense that a chair or a table is a thing. Like numerous other terms in common use, it cannot be defined by the simple, fundamental operation of "pointing at." It is not, we would insist, a directly denotable empirical datum, as such writers as Köhler (1929) have apparently maintained. But to deny to emotion the status of an immediately given simple real is not to imply that the concept is robbed of all scientific meaning or scientific reality. As Boring has observed:

Whatever exists as reality for psychology is a product of inductive inference—usually from experimental data. To say that these realities are hypothetical constructs is not to alter the truth. The atom is a construct and a reality. Its validity is attested by its power of physical subsumption. The realities are always tentative and have to make their way and prove their worth. They are as temporary as all truth. There is no other scientific meaning for reality.[1]

Thus, we would maintain that emotion is an inference or a scientific construct. Its scientific worth depends upon the degree to which it encompasses relationships among empirical events and thus leads to the more accurate understanding and prediction of behavior.

It has become apparent, furthermore, that at our present stage of theorizing in psychology, considerable progress toward the solution of vexing problems is promised by treating certain constructs as hypothetical variables intervening between environmental conditions and responses. It is in this way, we would suggest, that emotion (or emotions) might most profitably be conceptualized.[2]

The first outline of theoretical procedures explicitly involving hypothetical intervening variables in the formulation of psychological laws was presented by Tolman (1936). Subsequently, Hull (1943b) demonstrated the heuristic value of this conceptual device for the explanation of learning phenomena through the use of such constructs as habit, drive, and response evocation potentiality. Spence (1948) has likewise stressed the utility of intervening variables in theory construction and has sometimes referred to such variables as *calculational devices.* They are introduced for the express purpose of helping to account for behavioral phenomena. Their meaning derives solely from the logical, experimental, and computational operations that relate them to antecedent events, to presently acting stimulus conditions, and to responses.

Even if it be granted, however, that emotion, as a term in a science of behavior, should be regarded as a hypothetical intervening variable, the mere postulation of such a term constitutes only the beginning of a meaningful theory. Assuming that the primary concern of a science of psychology is the understanding of behavior at the molar level, then a large part of the psychologist's task is to delineate the factors that *function* as determinants of behavior. If emotion is to be included as one of the determinants, it is

---

[1] E. G. Boring, *The Physical Dimensions of Consciousness* (New York: Appleton-Century-Crofts, 1933), 7.
[2] In the present paper it has not seemed necessary to differentiate between *hypothetical constructs* and *intervening variables* in the manner suggested by MacCorquodale and Meehl (1948). For a critical evaluation of their view see Bergmann (1951).

imperative that a certain portion of a theory of emotion consist of hypotheses, or as Spence (1951) has termed them, "guesses at laws" concerning the functional relations between the hypothetical emotion and observable behavior. These guessed-at laws would be of the general form, "behavior is such and such a function of emotion or emotions." Such statements would specify the manner in which different intensities of one or more emotions function as differential determinants of behavior. By means of such functions some of the unexplained variability of behavior can be accounted for in terms of the concomitant variability in the hypothetical determining emotional state. This necessary process of working out the relations between emotion and observable behavior is referred to by Hull (1943b) as the anchoring of the construct to observable events on the consequent side.

But it is not sufficient to limit the treatment of emotion to statements concerning its inferential nature and to specifications of its hypothesized relations to overt behavior. It is also imperative that further specific guesses be hazarded by the theorist as to the manner in which variations in this hypothetical state are related to antecedent and current events and conditions, both external and internal. If such guesses are not made the theory is likely to be circular, in that variations in the state or process that are inferred from variations in behavior may in turn be used merely to account for these same behavioral variations. Tolman, Hull, and Spence have all explicitly and repeatedly emphasized the necessity for anchoring constructs to observable antecedent events. For example, Tolman, referring to Lewin's failure to carry out this important aspect of theorizing, says in part:

The conceptual system of topology and vectors obviously implies and requires in the end not only a set of principles whereby such and such individual and group life-space configurations will produce such and such behaviors but also *a set of principles whereby the independent variables of environmental situation and given personality make-up will produce such and such inner and outer life spaces.* And it is this latter set of principles which Lewin and his students, while not denying, seem to have been least explicit about stating.[3]

There is yet another requirement, however, that must be met by an acceptable theory. It is essential that the theory contain clear

[3] E. C. Tolman, "Kurt Lewin: 1890–1947," *Psychological Review,* 1948, **55**, 3–4. (Italics added.)

statements of the relationships existing between the construct of emotion and other constructs in the theoretical system. A theory of emotion has limited meaning apart from, and in the absence of, a logical and coherent statement of its relationships to the constructs embodied in more general theories of behavior. One must, we believe, specify in detail the relationship of the variable of emotion to such terms as habit, cognition, motivation, inhibition, or whatever other concepts one may prefer, for the process of fitting emotion into a broader systematic theory of behavior by determining its relations to the constructs of that theory constitutes the essence of what is involved in developing a theory of emotion.

To SUMMARIZE: A theory of emotion, stripped of its nonessentials, is simply a series of guesses as to the manner in which emotions are presumed to result from environmental events (past, present, internal, and external); guesses as to how they may resemble, differ from, and interact with other hypothetical states or processes within the organism; and guesses as to how different emotions, or differing degrees of the same emotion, may affect behavior differentially. It is furthermore stipulated that these various guessed-at relationships be stated specifically enough to assure their susceptibility to experimental test.

II. IMPLICATIONS OF THE SUGGESTED THEORETICAL APPROACH FOR SOME TRADITIONAL PROBLEMS OF EMOTION

A number of psychologists have advanced cogent arguments to support the contention that *emotion* is a superfluous term in psychology. Duffy (1934, 1948), for instance, has maintained—as have Meyer (1933) and Skinner (1938)—that emotional behavior differs only in degree from other kinds of behavior. She rejects the concept of emotion because she has been unable to discover any unique, qualitatively different properties of responses that can be unequivocally characterized as "emotional." Though we agree that it is probably impossible to distinguish between so-called emotional and nonemotional responses solely on the basis of their manifest descriptive characteristics, the present approach provides a quite different basis for deciding whether to retain or reject emotion as a distinctive construct. The criterion for making this decision inheres in the suggested requirement that the relations of emotion to other intervening variables in a broader behavioral theory be clearly delineated. *Emotion may be retained as a separate construct if, and only if, it is empirically useful to posit a state or process that is related to antecedent events, to other constructs, or to behavior by a different set of functions from those that characterize other constructs within the theory.* Thus, emotion and some other hypothetical state might have identical properties as behavior determinants and could not, therefore, be differentiated on the response side alone. Nevertheless, it might still be useful to conceive of their differing in respect of their antecedent conditions and (or) in respect of their relations to other constructs. From the present point of view, the problem is not whether emotion does or does not exist. It is a question, rather, of determining whether certain behavioral phenomena can be accounted for satisfactorily in terms of other well-established constructs. If such is not the case, then the introduction of additional "emotional" constructs may be worthwhile.

This line of reasoning is not, of course, restricted to emotion. It applies also to any other terms such as S-R *connection, expectancy, ego, attitude, perception, consciousness,* or *libido,* which one might wish to introduce into a systematic analysis of behavior. If the psychologist concerns himself with whether or not the ego, for instance, is "really there" in the organism, he is wasting his time. His proper concern is whether by introducing the term *ego,* by specifying that the ego varies in such and such a manner with observable antecedents, and by assuming that the ego determines behavior in specific ways, behavior can be more satisfactorily explained than if no ego is assumed.

Another implication of the present point of view is that the procedure of categorizing certain responses as emotional and others as nonemotional becomes unnecessary and undesirable. So far as we are aware, previous attempts to achieve such classificatory groupings have been notoriously futile. This is scarcely surprising, since it is hardly to be expected that a knowledge of only the observable features of a response would enable one to make accurate inferences about determining states that, by definition, can be inferred only from a knowledge of antecedent conditions, concomitant states, *and* responses. At any given instant, the topography of a given bit of behavior may reflect the action of numerous hypothetical determinants: habits, motivations, inhibitions, response-produced stimulations, perceptions, and (perhaps) emotions. More data than those provided by the topography of a response are needed to enable one to identify the extent of its dependence upon one rather than another of its many determinants. Skinner made this point a number of years ago when he asked: "Why should a certain part of the reactions of an organism be set aside in a special class? Why should we classify weeping in response to a bruised shin as emotional but weeping in response to a cinder in the eye as not?" [4] No satisfactory answers to these questions have apparently been suggested.

Psychologists who deal primarily with so-called nonemotional behavior seem less frequently concerned with problems of response categorization than those who deal largely with emotions. In the absence of information about antecedent conditions or environmental events, the learning theorist does not ordinarily ask whether a specific response is due, say, to a habit rather than a drive, nor usually whether it is due to one drive rather than another. Were he to do so, he would undoubtedly encounter the same difficulties that have beset students of emotion. For example, if one notes that an animal eats greedily of moist food, one might ask whether the animal is hungry or thirsty. From observations of eating behavior alone, this question could never be answered since this response, like most others, may be evoked as a result of learning, in the presence of any one of a variety of drives. In the foregoing example, it is even possible that the animal—and this seems to be occasionally true of humans also—is neither hungry nor thirsty but anxious. Information to the effect that the animal had been supplied with food but no water, or the reverse, might enable the observer to make a decision in this instance; but, for the most part, such a discovery would be of much less interest than the determination of the functional relations between the time or kind of deprivation on the one hand and such variables as the rate, latency, or resistance to extinction of eating on the other.

Finally, the traditional problem of determining how many basically different emotions "exist" is from the present viewpoint similar to that of determining whether *any* emotion "exists." The classical approach involved attempts to determine the number of different emotions that could be accurately identified from facial expressions or teased out by painstaking microanalyses of conscious contents. All efforts to reach agreements by these methods have

[4] B. F. Skinner, *The Behavior of Organisms* (New York: Appleton-Century-Crofts, 1938), 406.

apparently ended in failure. More progress might have been made if it had been asked instead whether observable behavior is most satisfactorily explained by the introduction of one or more constructs carrying an emotional label. If it appears desirable to have more than one, each must be shown to have relations that are in some way distinctive with reference to the other elements of the theory and to each other. Different emotions exist as realities for psychology only if different defining operations and interrelations can be clearly specified for them. If such specifications cannot be made the superfluous terms are scientifically inadmissable and must be coalesced or deleted; appeals for their continuance on intuitive or phenomenological grounds must be rejected. A situation of exactly this sort faces us at the present time in respect to the constructs of conflict and frustration. But a discussion of this problem will be postponed until we have had an opportunity to examine briefly some current conceptions of emotion in the light of the analyses presented above.

✻   ✻   ✻

IV. Nonemotional Interpretations of Frustration Behavior

In order to exemplify the proposed methods of attacking the problem of emotion, the remainder of this paper is devoted to a consideration of phenomena commonly attributed to the "emotion" of frustration. Our principal objective in what follows is the presentation (Section V) of a paradigmatic theory involving the postulation of a special "emotional state" of frustration. But an adequate evaluation of such a theory cannot be made unless some attention is also given to *nonemotional* explanations of the same phenomena. The present section is devoted, therefore, to a brief examination of interpretations of frustration behavior founded primarily upon conventional learning principles. Our selection of frustration for detailed consideration does not involve the assumption that events usually included under this heading are entirely representative of all events to which the term *emotion* has been applied.

Perhaps the most prevalent assumption about frustration is that it results whenever conditions are such as to hinder or prevent the occurrence of a response. Typically, it is also posited that the responding organism is motivated to make the response, that the response is (or has in the past been) instrumental to the achievement of a goal and that stimuli normally capable of eliciting the blocked response are acting upon the organism. Under conditions of this general sort various types of behavior may be exhibited. Among those frequently reported are: responses of a trial-and-error type directed toward the surmounting of an obstacle, responses of escaping from the frustrating situation, more persistent or vigorous counterparts of the originally blocked responses, aggressive responses, and so-called disorganized responses. . . .

. . . It would appear, therefore, that there is a high degree of correspondence between frustrating and problem-solving situations, and the reactions observed to occur therein; consequently it might be supposed that explanatory concepts appropriate to the one might also fit the other. Significantly, learning theorists have typically not found it necessary to employ emotional concepts in their interpretations of problem-solving behavior. Rather, they are likely to appeal to the effects of previous experiences (in the same or similar situations), to innate predispositions, to antecedent conditions of deprivation, and the like. To a degree, then, many learning theorists may be regarded as proponents of nonemotional interpretations of frustration. . . .

. . . Such anlyses as these indicate that nonemotional interpretations may prove adequate to explain a good deal of behavior following blocking. Nevertheless, the possibility remains that a theoretical schema involving the concept of emotion would be more satisfactory. For instance, it may be useful to suppose that thwarting leads to an increase in motivation in order to explain frustration-produced phenomena such as those described clinically as "overcompensation." Such an assumption might also serve as the basis for the notion that escape from a thwarting situation is reinforcing, quite independently of the instrumental function of such escape in reducing some other drive. Finally, the observation that thwarting is accompanied by or leads to rather unique kinds of responses such as aggression, which appear inappropriate to or independent of specific stimulus conditions, might argue for the desirability of postulating an emotional process.[5] In the following section, therefore, a tentative "emotional" theory of frustration behavior is presented as a possible alternative to "nonemotional" interpretations of the type considered here.

[5] It should be observed that a demonstration of the utility of adding new constructs or of changing old ones does not invalidate a given theoretical approach in its entirety. One may consider in this regard the manner in which the concept of anxiety, which is strongly connotative of emotionality, has been added to and incorporated within the general framework of Hullian theory.

V. An "Emotional" Interpretation of Frustration Behavior

In the interest of terminological clarity, it should be stressed at the outset that the term *frustration,* as used here, refers to a hypothetical (defined) state or condition of an organism. It is to be distinguished, therefore, from a *frustrating event* such as the blocking or nonrewarding of a response. Unfortunately, the term *frustration* has been used in the past to mean either a state induced by a frustrating event or the frustrating event itself, or both. The terms *anger* or *annoyance* might be substituted for frustration provided they are divested of their classical attributes as unique conscious *quale* or immediately given phenomenological entities.

Since it is our contention that theories of emotion have little meaning apart from more comprehensive theories of behavior, the present treatment has been coordinated with Hull's system as presented in the *Principles of Behavior* (1943b). Insofar as space permits, the ways in which the present construct of frustration and its relations resemble or differ from those proposed by Hull are indicated in a general manner. Our preference for a formulation of a concept of frustration within the framework of Hullian theory in no sense implies that it could not be treated, perhaps equally well, in terms of other thoretical systems.

If the procedures suggested in the earlier sctions of this paper are to be followed, the *initial* tasks in outlining a theory of frustration must be (1) the denotation of the antecedent conditions that are assumed to lead to frustration, and (2) the specification of the functional relations holding between frustration and these conditions. The first three of the following subsections are devoted to these tasks.

Antecedents to Frustration.   As we have already noted, a common assumption made by writers in this area is that frustration develops under any condition that hinders or prevents the occurrence of a response to which there is a supraliminal excitatory tendency. With this assumption as a starting point, a number of different kinds of manipulable conditions may be defined as antecedents to frustration. Among these are (1) the introduction of partial or complete physical barriers; (2) the introduction of delay periods between the initiation and completion of a response sequence; (3) the omission or reduction of a customary reward on one or more trials; and (4) variations in the organism's condition, environment, or training leading to the evocation of a response tendency that is incompatible with an ongoing one.

Although these antecedents differ widely with respect to their manifest topographical features, the capacity they possess in common to thwart an ongoing response may be accounted for by assuming that *each functions in some way to arouse an incompatible reaction tendency.* These competitive tendencies may be either positive excitatory tendencies to perform a conflicting response or inhibitory tendencies such as those resulting from the expenditure of effort. The basic assumption is made, therefore, that *frustration is the consequence of either (1) the simultaneous activation of two competing excitatory tendencies, or (2) the presence of a single excitatory tendency and an opposing inhibitory tendency.*[6]

The exact manner in which any particular antecedent might lead to an opposing tendency and the nature of the tendency aroused in each case can only be surmised at present. If an organism has been trained to approach a spatially remote goal and is then hindered by a physical barrier from reaching that goal, it is conceivable that the original approach tendency would be opposed by both excitatory and inhibitory tendencies. For an organism that has had prior experiences in similar thwarting situations the mere sight of the barrier could elicit incompatible excitatory tendencies to retreat. Or, the barrier might lead to an increase in reactive inhibition if it occasioned vigorous and repeated barrier-circumventing reactions. Frustration resulting from the introduction of delay periods is attributable to decreased effectiveness of reinforcement and therefore to smaller increments in excitatory tendency in the face of undiminished increments in work inhibition. Indeed, the increments of inhibition may actually increase, since, in practice, delays are nearly always produced by increasing the distance from the start to the

---

[6] In view of the fact that the oppositional nature of these antecedents is stressed, whether they result from excitatory or inhibitory tendencies, it may be reasonably argued that they should be regarded as *conflict* situations, or in our terminology, antecedents to a hypothetical state of conflict. We do not believe, however, that a useful division can be made at present between conflict and frustration. If one wishes, one might define the state induced by the first kind of antecedent (competing $_s E_R$) described above as conflict, and the second (competing I_R) as frustration. But so far as we are aware, no one has formulated a distinction between the two constructs of frustration and conflict that rests in a convincing way upon demonstrable differences in their functional relations to other constructs or to behavior.

goal or by introducing a physical barrier. In either case, the procedures used to produce delays might provide additional stimuli which could function to elicit or facilitate positive competing tendencies. The way in which nonreinforced trials are conceived to produce frustration depends on one's conception of the nature of the extinction process. Within Hull's theory, reactive inhibition (I_R) is assigned the principal role, though provision is also made for the learning of competing habits ($_sI_R$'s). Finally, all the operations by which an organism's condition, environment, or previous training are manipulated so as to facilitate the evocation of an incompatible response are presumed to lead to frustration mainly through the concurrent activation of competing excitatory tendencies.

The hypothesis that frustration develops under conditions that hinder or prevent the occurrence of a response is a definition of the same general order as Hull's definition of drive in terms of antecedent conditions of deprivation. But unelaborated definitions of this sort have limited applicability. Unless frustration is to be conceived as an all-or-none event, the assumed functional relationship of frustration to its antecedents must be stated more precisely. To do this, both the breadth and the specificity of our assumptions must be increased.

THE MAGNITUDES OF THE EXCITATORY AND INHIBITORY COMPETITIVE TENDENCIES AS FUNCTIONS OF THEIR ANTECEDENTS. Since the assumption has been made that frustration results from the competition of reaction tendencies, and since these tendencies, like frustration, are constructs, it is evident that one of the first tasks is to indicate the ways in which the magnitudes of these hypothetical variables might vary with changes in observable events. Until this has been accomplished, and the further relation of frustration to the competitive tendencies has been outlined, frustration itself cannot be related to manipulable antecedents.

In situations in which the antecedent conditions lead to the elicitation (or strengthening) or a conflicting *excitatory* tendency, the problem of specifying the relations between the observable independent variables and the strength of the competitive tendency is identical with that of accounting for the strength of any response tendency whatsoever. Following Hull, it may be assumed that the competitive excitatory potential ($_sE_R$) is determined by the multiplicative combination of habit strength of the ($_sH_R$) and effective drive ($\overline{D}$). Consequently the strength of the $_sE_R$ may be assumed to vary in some such manner as Hull suggests with number of re-inforced trials, amount of reward, delay of reinforcement, strength of drive, and so on. Since these conditions determine the strengths of both the thwarted and thwarting tendencies they constitute the effective antecedents to frustration when two incompatible responses are instigated.

In situations in which frustration results from the negative effect of *inhibition*,[7] the strength of the inhibition may be assumed to be a function of the degree of work involved in executing the thwarted response and the number of times the response is elicited. Here Hull has proposed as a specific hypothesis that $I_R = cn/B - W$, where n is the number of response evocations, c and B are constants, and W represents work measured in physical units (Hull, 1943b). By this equation, if work per trial is held constant, inhibition increases linearly with number of trials; and if the number of trials is held constant, a positively accelerated curve of inhibition is obtained with increases in amount of work. If an additional simplifying assumption is made that amount of work is linearly related to degree of blocking and length of delay, the relation of inhibition to these antecedents and to the number of response evocations might be given to a first approximation by Hull's equation.

Up to this point it has been assumed that the magnitude of frustration is some function of the respective strengths of simultaneously aroused competitive tendencies, and that the strengths of these tendencies may be inferred from Hull's assumptions regarding the specific observable variables influencing the development of excitatory and inhibitory tendencies. The next step is to delineate the functional relations that might obtain between frustration and the competitive tendencies.

FRUSTRATION AS A JOINT FUNCTION OF THE ABSOLUTE AND RELATIVE STRENGTHS OF THE THWARTED AND COMPETING TENDENCIES. In writings on frustration and conflict two rather frequent, though by no means always explicit, suggestions may be found as to the manner in which frustration or conflict might vary with the strengths of two competing tendencies. It has been assumed (1) that frustra-

[7] In this section, the terms *inhibitory tendency* or *inhibition* refer to any state or condition of the organism (other than a competing excitatory tendency) that tends to produce a cessation of a given activity. They correspond roughly to Hull's concept of *reactive inhibition* (I_R). Although Hull's total inhibitory potential (I_R) also includes a conditioned component ($_sI_R$) no attempt is made here to consider the possible influence of this latter factor.

tion increases as the difference between the strengths of the tendencies is reduced, being maximal at the point of equality, and (2) that if the two tendencies are equally strong, then the greater their absolute strengths, the more intense the frustration. Although there are some experimental data that lend credibility to each of these assumptions separately, the factors involved have not been integrated into a single principle encompassing their joint operation or interaction. For instance, one cannot predict on the basis of the separate assumptions whether two weak tendencies that differ by a given amount will produce the same degree of frustration as two stronger tendencies differing by a greater amount.

One specific hypothesis with respect to the relation of frustration (F) to both the relative and absolute strengths of two competing tendencies may be expressed by the formula

$$F = \frac{E_w{}^n}{E_s{}^{n-1}}$$

where $E_w{}^n$ is the weaker of the two tendencies (either an $_sE_R$ or an I_R) raised to the nth power, and $E_s{}^{n-1}$ is the stronger tendency (presumably always an $_sE_R$) raised to the n − 1th power.[8] If n is set at unity, F becomes directly proportional to the strength of the weaker tendency alone, since the denominator reduces to unity. It is notable that this specific assumption, though couched in different terms, has already been made by French (1944). His proposal thus emerges as a special case of the one suggested here. On his hypothesis, however, neither the absolute strength of the stronger tendency nor the relative strengths of the two tendencies can enter into the determination of frustration. Assuming that such factors as these are important, it is necessary to set n at some value greater than 1 so the F will decrease with departures from equality produced either by increasing E_s (with E_w constant) or by decreasing E_w (with E_s constant). . . .

. . . The following relations may be noted:

[8] It should be perfectly clear that this particular hypothesis and the specific numerical values employed throughout this presentation have been arbitrarily selected to facilitate the process of exposition. No one would be more surprised than we if these particular hypothetical relations should prove to be exactly the ones that best predict empirical findings in this area. We merely wish to illustrate in an admittedly schematic and incomplete way the kind of quantification of variables and specification of relations that is required, according to our conception, in any serious attempt to formulate an "emotional" (or, indeed, any other) theory of frustration.

1. An increase in the strength of the competitive tendency (E_w) with the dominant tendency (E_s) held constant, or a decrease in the strength of E_s with E_w fixed, results in a positively accelerated increase in frustration (F) which reaches its maximum value when $E_s = E_w$. That is, if either of the two tendencies remains unchanged, frustration increases as the difference between them is reduced.

2. Conversely any increase in the difference between the strengths of the two tendencies will result in a decrease in frustration regardless of whether E_s is increased relative to E_w or whether E_w is decreased relative to E_s. These two implications are congruent with the first of the general assumptions about frustration noted at the beginning of this section.

3. Simultaneous increases in the strengths of both tendencies will produce increasingly greater values of frustration provided the increases are such as to maintain either the ratio of the tendencies or their absolute difference constant. In either instance, the relations between frustration and the strength of either of the two tendencies will be linear. . . . This implication relates to the second general assumption mentioned above.

If our initial guesses regarding the relations of the competitive tendencies to their antecedents are now considered in conjunction with the proposed equation for frustration, it becomes possible to formulate a number of specific hypotheses concerning the effect of number of nonreinforced trials, changes in length of delay, degree of blocking, and the like, upon degree of frustration. For example, let it be assumed that I_R increases linearly with successive nonreinforced trials and that the thwarted E_s remains unchanged. It then follows from our equation (by treating I_R as equivalent to E_w) that F will increase in a positively accelerated manner with successive extinction trials. Or again, let it be supposed the E_w increases in a negatively accelerated manner as a function of the number of reinforcements of the habit involved. In this case if E_s remains constant, it can be shown that the curve for the growth of F as a function of successive reinforcements of the weaker habit will have a predominantly negatively accelerated form but with a slight positive initial acceleration. Such hypotheses as these cannot be tested, however, until additional assumptions have been made concerning the relations of frustration to constructs such as habit and drive and, particularly, to overt behavior.

THE RELATION OF FRUSTRATION TO THE THEORETICAL CONSTRUCTS OF HABIT ($_sH_R$) AND DRIVE (D). When the competitive tendencies are both excitatory potentials, it follows from Hull's equation for $_sE_R$ (1943b) that each tendency is determined by its corresponding habit strength ($_sH_R$) and by the effective drive state ($\overline{D}$) which is common to both. Thus,

$$_sE_R = \frac{S^HR \times \overline{D}}{100}$$

From this relation, it can be seen that changes in the strengths of either the habits or of the drive will affect the magnitude of frustration. With $\overline{D}$ held constant, an increase in the stronger habit or a decrease in the weaker will decrease frustration; conversely, decreasing the stronger habit or increasing the weaker will increase frustration. If the strengths of *both* habits are varied, frustration may either increase or decrease, depending on the direction and extent of the changes. When the two habits (whether equal or unequal) are held constant, however, frustration will increase with heightened drive and decrease with reduced drive.[9] This holds even though increased drive magnifies the absolute difference between initially unequal excitatory tendencies. Since the numerator is squared in the suggested equation for frustration, any change in drive affects its value more than it does that of the denominator.

Where the weaker of the two opposing tendencies is *inhibitory* rather than *excitatory* the present theory suggests that the effects of motivational changes may be different. If I_R is unaffected by changes in $\overline{D}$, as Hull assumes, and if I_R is substituted for E_w in the equation for F, then raising the value of $\overline{D}$ will heighten E_s only and thereby *reduce* F. Increasing $\overline{D}$ in this situation is therefore functionally equivalent to increasing E_s with E_w held constant. However, it should be noted that an intense drive could lead to more frequent and more vigorous responses of attacking a barrier and hence to the accumulation of more inhibition than would occur

[9] This deduction regarding the expected effect upon frustration of an increase in motivation is supported by Finch's experimental observations (1942) and by both theoretical and experimental conclusions from the Yale studies of frustration (Dollard *et al.*, 1939). Thus, Dollard and his colleagues have assumed that the strength of instigation to aggression (which is roughly equivalent to what is meant here by strength of frustration) varies directly with the strength of instigation to the frustrated response (similar to strength of $\overline{D}$ in our present usage).

under a weak drive. Such an increase in I_R might raise the ratio I_R/E_s to a value equal to or conceivably even greater than that obtaining under a lower drive. In this manner, F might be intensified by increasing $\bar{D}$ even under conditions of competition by an inhibitory state.

Some of the suggested relations between frustration and other constructs may now be summarized. Since frustration is assumed to vary as a function of drive intensity it bears some resemblance to Hull's concept of excitatory potential. The two differ, however, not only in terms of their consequences, but also in terms of their relations on the antecedent side. If drive is held constant, frustration increases with the number of nonreinforced trials, whereas $_s\bar{E}_R$ remains unchanged. (Hull's *effective* excitatory potential, $_s\bar{E}_R$, decreases under such circumstances since $_s\bar{E}_R = {}_sE_R - \dot{I}_R$.) Moreover, although both frustration and inhibition increase with the number of nonreinforced trials, their rates of growth as functions of increases in the value of this variable follow different laws, and their respective effects upon behavior are also assumed to be different.

Frustration as a determinant of behavior. The final step in our theoretical outline is to suggest ways in which the postulated frustration state might significantly affect overt behavior. From the hypotheses of other writers and from additional considerations, two likely possibilities emerge: (1) that frustration increases the general level of motivation, and (2) that frustration produces, or is accompanied by, unique internal stimuli.

The possibility that frustration leads to a heightened drive level is clearly coordinate with the notion that emotions have motivational properties, with current conceptions of the drive properties of fear and anxiety, and with numerous, though somewhat unsystematic observations of a clinical nature. Perhaps the most feasible method of incorporating this supposition into Hull's theory would be to assume that frustration-produced drive has *the functional status of an irrelevant drive.* According to Hull, irrelevant drives combine with primary drives to produce the effective drive ($\bar{D}$) that energizes habits into action. On this assumption, the presence of frustration should produce an increment in an organism's effective level of motivation. It follows from this that responses elicited at the time frustration is aroused, or shortly thereafter, should be more intense than those elicited when frustration is absent. Moreover, if a response is followed by a reduction in frustration the tendency to perform that response should be strengthened, since drive reduction is assumed to be reinforcing. . . .

. . . It may be observed here that although motivational properties have been attributed to frustration, *it differs from other drives such as hunger and thirst in its presumed dependence upon the arousal of competitive tendencies rather than upon conditions of deprivation. It also differs from other motivational states with respect to the events that result in its diminution.* Frustration, by assumption, is reduced by increasing the strength of the stronger tendency, by decreasing the strength of the weaker, by allowing fatigue effects to dissipate, and so on. Clearly these are not operations commonly supposed to reduce the strength of other drives. In these several additional respects, therefore, the present construct of frustration satisfies the requirement that it have guessed-at relations differing from those obtaining for other constructs already in systematic use.

The second major role that frustration might play in determining behavior is by functioning as a stimulus. If at the time that competing tendencies are aroused, unique, differentiable, internal stimuli are generated, the organism's behavior might be affected in a variety of ways. First, such stimuli could provide the means whereby an organism might learn to discriminate between (react differentially to) frustration and other states such as fear or hunger. Secondly, frustration-produced stimuli might, as the result of innately established connections, elicit specific overt responses or response patterns quite unlike those aroused under other antecedent conditions. Frustration might thus serve as an important *source of new response patterns.* Finally, the attributing of stimulus properties to frustration might provide an acceptable explanation of the fact that so-called emotional responses often seem irrelevant and inappropriate to the immediate external situation in which they occur. If a distinctive response were associated, either innately or through learning, with frustration-produced stimuli, it could appear in a wide variety of different situations, providing they all result in frustration. Responses to frustration originally restricted to a single environmental context might thus be elicited by frustration-produced cues in other contexts, despite any ostensible inappropriateness that might characterize such appearances.

Although certain acts might depend initially upon the stimuli accompanying frustration, the mere occurrence of such responses

may not always imply the presence of frustration. Like any unconditioned response, a frustration reaction might become conditioned to
other (perhaps external) "nonfrustration" stimuli. If so, it could
presumably be evoked by these neutral stimuli even in the absence
of frustration. This possibility is consistent with our contention that
useful inferences as to the presence of frustration must rest upon
data other than those obtained from observations of so-called emotional reactions alone.

It will be apparent from this treatment of frustration as a determinant of behavior that no attempt has been made to specify
precisely which responses will appear in thwarting situations. The
present theory does lead to the expectations that the presence of
frustration will often result in the intensification of responses, that
reactions followed by a reduction in frustration will be reinforced,
and that responses associated with frustration in one situation will
tend to appear in other thwarting situations. But there is nothing in
the theory itself to imply that aggression, for instance, will occur
more frequently than withdrawal, or withdrawal more frequently
than, say, primitivization. That this is not necessarily a weakness of
the theory is suggested by the following considerations.

1. In the first place, an important role is assigned in our treatment
to the operation of learning factors. Thus it has been hypothesized
that many "nonemotional" responses can become conditioned to
frustration-generated, as well as to external, stimuli. And conversely,
originally innate reactions to frustration are thought to be capable
of becoming functionally connected to almost any stimulus. Starting
from such assumptions, it is impossible to anticipate the occurrence
of specific responses in the absence of either detailed learning histories for each individual or normative data with respect to cultural
determinants of responses and reinforcements. The theory could be
altered, of course, to include an assumption that aggression, or some
other type of behavior, is an innately determined consequent of
frustration. But since a wide variety of different responses have
been observed to accompany frustration it seems highly unlikely,
in the case of human behavior at least, that responses to frustration
are genetically determined to any important degree.

2. In the second place, an implicit assumption (following Hull)
of the present theory is that when two or more response tendencies
are simultaneously incited, the one having the greatest momentary
strength will be revealed in action, though the vigor, latency, and

frequency of the reaction may be modified by the competing tendency. Furthermore, different kinds of competing tendencies may also be expected to affect differentially the qualitative characteristics of reactions to frustration. If a rat is frustrated while running it may respond quite differently from one that is frustrated while pressing a lever. In human subjects, the blocking of gross muscular activity may lead to quite different behavior than does the thwarting of verbal activity. In general, then, we would suppose that actions attending frustration will vary with the nature of the responses evoked by the task or activity in progress. Only from a knowledge of the relative strengths of the response tendencies and their degree of incompatibility could the occurrence of a specific response be predicted.

3. As a final point, it may be observed that the assumed effects upon performance of changes in motivation are such as to impose definite restrictions on our ability to predict frustration reactions. Within the theoretical structure adopted, an increase in motivation will (by virtue of its postulated multiplicative action) increase the absolute difference between two initially unequal excitatory tendencies, providing neither is already at or near its maximum. An increase in motivation due to frustration may lead, therefore, either to better performance, if the "correct" tendency is strongest, or to poorer performance, if the "incorrect" tendency is dominant. We must know in advance what the relative strengths of these tendencies are likely to be if the outcome of frustration is to be predicted in any rigorous fashion. And even this is an over-simplification, since further complexities may result from the elicitation of potentially competitive responses by frustration itself. . . .

. . . The adequacy of this particular theory in accounting for the behavioral phenomena so often attributed to the emotion of frustration is an empirical question. It is admittedly incomplete and in some important aspects more obscure than any respectable theory ought to be. Nevertheless, even in this sketchy form, it appears capable of generating a number of deductions that could be put to empirical test. We have no doubt that such tests may indicate the necessity for extensive modification of this theory. Perhaps the facts will even require its abandonment. But, of course, it is precisely this vulnerability to experimental attack that constitutes the end to which our suggested criteria of an acceptable theory of emotion have been proposed.

[7]

Frustrative Nonreward in Partial Reinforcement and Discrimination Learning: Some Recent History and a Theoretical Extension [1]

ABRAM AMSEL

The overall objective of this paper is to examine the current status of a concept of frustrative nonreward in behavior theory. The examination takes two forms: a general discussion and survey of recent work on motivating and inhibiting properties of nonreward, followed by a theoretical extension of frustrative-nonreward theory to certain prediscrimination phenomena.

In the first part of the paper a brief historical account will be presented of recent changes toward an "active" conceptualization of nonreward, particularly in neo-Hullian theory, the current status of such an active nonreward concept in explanations of partial reinforcement effects will be set in a broader framework of partial reinforcement theories, and some recent data will be presented in support of the idea that discrimination learning involves frustrative-nonreward effects.

The second more theoretical portion of this paper stems from an earlier frustrative conceptualization of nonreward (Amsel, 1958). It represents an attempt to extend frustrative-nonreward theory to situations in which discrimination learning is preceded by various amounts and kinds of "prior experience." These prior experiences will be termed "Prediscrimination treatments" and will involve training to approach in the the presence of one or both (separately)

[1] A shorter version of this paper was presented to the Psychology Colloquium of the University of Illinois in May 1961. The preparation of this paper and much of the experimental research to which it refers were supported by grants (G–5527 and G–13895) from the National Science Foundation.

SOURCE: Abram Amsel, "Frustrative Nonreward in Partial Reinforcement and Discrimination Learning: Some Recent History and a Theoretical Extension," *Psychological Review*, 1962, **69**, 306–328. Reprinted by permission of the American Psychological Association and Abram Amsel.

of the eventual discriminanda, under conditions of partial or of continuous reinforcement.

HISTORY

Hull's adoption of what he termed the Mowrer-Miller hypothesis as a basis for a two-factor theory of inhibition (Hull, 1943b) was, at the time, the acceptance of a "passive" conception of nonreward and rejection of a more active conception which he and others had held. Certainly, Pavlov's nonreinforcement, producing internal inhibition, was an active conception. Spence's (1936, 1937) theory of discrimination learning, clearly in the Pavlovian tradition, also assigned special inhibitory properties to nonreinforcement. In some of his more recent systematic writing, Spence (1956) points out that his position on the Mowrer-Miller hypothesis was never in agreement with Hull's.

Emotional-motivational effects of nonreward, as they relate to learning, were described in an article by Miller and Stevenson (1936), which attributed the agitated behavior of rats during extinction to effects of nonreinforcement carried over from one trial to the next. This is an example of an active motivational conception of nonreward. A similar emotional-motivational interpretation of nonreward can be found in Skinner (1938).

In Hull's 1943 theory, which dominated the psychology of learning in the forties, nonreinforcement was an event without direct inhibitory or motivational effect as it was also in the early mathematical-model treatments of learning (Bush & Mosteller, 1951; Estes, 1950). By about 1950, however, expressions of dissatisfaction with the passive theoretical status of nonreward were emerging. These expressions were in theoretically oriented experiments and in theoretical papers. Most of the early defections from 1943 Hull, in this connection, were by persons close to the Hullian point of view. There are suggestions that Hull, himself, was getting ready to change his position on this shortly before his death.[2]

Rohrer's (1949) treatment of extinction in terms of a "frustration drive" was one of the first expressions of a desire to give nonreinforcement a more active role in inhibition.[3] However, while Rohrer's

[2] See C. L. Hull, *A Behavior System* (New Haven: Yale University Press, 1952), Ch. 5.
[3] It is questionable that *inhibition* is the appropriate and correct term to use in regard to response decrement related to frustrative nonreward. Better terms

reference to frustration was specifically related to the operation of nonreinforcement, it provided no particular mechanism for frustrative inhibition. At about the same time, the well-known experiments of Virginia Sheffield (1949, 1950) appeared, relating partial reinforcement acquisition and extinction effects to the spacing of trials and containing suggestions of both frustration drive and frustrative inhibition. These articles and another by Stanley (1952), along with a late experimental paper by Hull and others (Hull, Livingston, Rouse, & Barker, 1951) and Hull's (1952) last book, all contained at least the germ of a change toward a more active conception of nonreinforcement. An experimental paper by Denny and Dunham (1951) offered inhibition based on nonreinforcement (frustration) as an alternative to reactive inhibition to account for differential nonreinforcement effects in a T maze.

Brown and Farber (1951) outlined a theory in which nonreward was one of several antecedents to frustration. In this paper, the major emphasis was on the definition of frustration in terms of competing response tendencies and the authors were concerned only with the motivational (drive) properties of frustration, and not with inhibitory effects. In the same year, a paper by Amsel (1951) made the point that fractional anticipatory frustration (r_F), which is the classically conditioned form of the frustrative reaction to nonreward, provides a mechanism for conceptualizing the active properties of nonreinforcement and should be regarded as a determiner of inhibitory effects. And, at about the same time, Seward (1951) published a theoretical paper which mentioned, without elaboration, the possible functional properties of an anticipatory frustration factor.

The remainder of the decade, 1950 to 1960, has seen a number of additional experimental and theoretical attacks on the problem of nonreward. On the one hand there are experiments and theoretical treatments by investigators in the Hullian tradition of behavior theory which have sought to extend and revise Hull's theory in regard to the status of nonreward. The other hand holds a number of published studies representing a variety of theoretical and nontheoretical interests which have contributed information about frustrative nonreward.

---

would be *interference* or *competition,* since frustrative inhibition cannot be regarded as directly affecting the excitatory tendency out of which it grows. It is rather a new excitatory tendency which competes with the older one.

Much of this work has been reviewed earlier (Amsel, 1958; Lawson & Marx, 1958a); but some of it is very recent. The experiments fall into three categories: (a) demonstrations of the motivating effects of frustrative nonreward, i.e., the carried-over, enhancing effect of nonreward on the vigor of immediately following behavior. This has been termed the Frustration Effect (FE). Several studies, by far the greatest number, have been directed not only at demonstrating the effect but also at examining the variables determining its occurrence and strength (Amsel, Ernhart, & Galbrecht, 1961; Amsel & Hancock, 1957; Amsel & Penick, 1962; Amsel & Roussel, 1952; Bower & Stocks, 1960; Longstreth, 1960; Marzocco, 1950; Penney, 1960; Roussel, 1952; Seward, Pereboom, Butler, & Jones, 1957; Wagner, 1959). (b) The second category consists of experiments which are mainly concerned with the frustration drive stimulus, but which also touch on frustration reduction as reinforcement (Amsel & Prouty, 1959; Amsel & Ward, 1954; Tyler, Marx, & Collier, 1959). (c) And finally, there are a few studies which deal with the inhibitory properties of frustrative nonreward. The inhibitory mechanism is fractional anticipatory frustration (r_F), a classically conditioned form of the goal response to frustrative nonreward. The mechanism and its theoretical properties have been identified in detail (Amsel, 1958; Spence, 1960), and experiments testing implications of such a mechanism are available (Bower, 1961; Goodrich, 1959; Haggard, 1959; Wagner, 1961a, 1961b). Of particular importance in this connection are a series of experiments by Wagner (1961b) which go far toward establishing the proposition that frustrative nonreward has many of the properties of punishment, and that r_F operates in many respects like fear. These experiments would support such statements as (a) the greater the strength of frustration, the faster the extinction (avoidance) of a nonrewarded response; (b) cues paired with frustrative nonreward acquire motivational properties; and (c) the cessation of cues previously paired with frustrative nonreward serves to reinforce a new response.

There are several other experiments on nonreward (or reward prevention) as a variable in learning which provide support for nonreward as a factor in inhibition. For example, studies by Lambert and Solomon (1952) and by Adelman and Rosenbaum (1954) related extinction to the blocking of instrumental behavior at various distances from the goal. An experiment by Adelman and Maatsch

(1955) found that resistance to extinction depends to some extent on what the subject is allowed to do when it finds no reward in the goal box, i.e., is frustrated. The suggestion is that resistance to extinction is high when the subject makes a response to frustration which removes it from the frustrating situation rather than one which keeps it in the apparatus. Ferster (1957, 1958) found that stimuli signaling "time out" from positive reinforcement acquire aversive properties. He also showed that the withdrawal of a positive conditioned reinforcer had the functional properties of punishment, suppressing the rate of responding much like the presence of a negative reinforcer. These experiments point clearly to the inhibitory (aversive) properties of nonreward.

Some recent experiments, which show decreasing resistance to extinction with increasing numbers and magnitudes of reinforcement, must be regarded as supporting a conception of nonreward as an active factor. For example, Hulse (1958) and Armus (1959) found that larger magnitudes of reinforcement in acquisition are followed by faster extinction. Very recent reports by Reynolds and Siegel (1961), by Pavlik (1961), and by Wagner (1961a) were to the same effect. North and Stimmel (1960) have shown that rats reinforced 90 or 135 times extinguish faster than those reinforced 45 times. Similar results have been reported by Reynolds, Richter, and Carlock (1960). They found faster extinction following .5- and following .1-gram reward, and faster extinction after 66 acquisition trials than after 6, 12, or 30 trials. This kind of result is quite in accord with results from studies of overlearning and discrimination reversal, which we will look at later. Together, they are as incompatible with early Hullian theory, or any other theory requiring monotonicity and positive relationships in these variables (e.g., the various mathematical approaches), as were the early partial reinforcement findings. We will come back to some of these experiments later, and my discussion of partial reinforcement effects will show why a theory which includes a frustrative nonreward hypothesis must predict such results.

There are by now several experiments which can be taken to indicate that nonreinforcement is more important than reinforcement in discrimination. Chronologically these are studies by Fitzwater (1952), Grove and Eninger (1952), Eninger (1953), Shoemaker (1953), Cantor and Spiker (1954), Grice and Goldman

(1955), Birch (1955), and Solomon (1956), to mention some of the earlier ones. A very recent study which makes this same point has been reported by Lachman (1961). This is not the place for a detailed description of these studies; however, the burden of evidence is that avoidance of nonreward is a more powerful factor in discrimination than approach to reward; and this is, of course, very relevant to a point of view which makes nonreward a determiner of inhibition. Perhaps Harlow and Hicks (1957) were reacting not only to their own experimental findings but also to the weight of this kind of evidence when they argued for a "uniprocess" rather than a "duoprocess" theory of discrimination learning, the single process being inhibition. The weakness of their argument is that the negative process (r_F, in my terms) may well depend on the prior existence of a positive process (see Amsel, 1958; Spence, 1936, 1937), and one is back to two processes again.

Other examples of a return to an active conception of nonreward outside of the Hull-Spence camp can be found in the recent work of Mowrer and Estes. Mowrer, in his *Learning Theory and Behavior,* makes frequent use of the notion of nongoal events arousing "frustration" or "anger," in addition to "disappointment," and expresses agreement with the position I favor in regard to frustrative goal events.[4] Estes (1959) has recently acknowledged that statistical learning theory must cope with the problem of an active negative process based on nonreward in these words:

. . . I have found that in the naive animal an unreinforced trial produces no apparent change in response probabilities, but that after a series of reinforced runs to a given side of a T maze, the introduction of non-reinforcement yields a decrement in probability of response to that side . . . Apparently under partial reinforcement schedules, the effect of non-reinforcement varies between these extremes. . . .[5]

From this brief sketch of the recent history of the concept of nonreward, we move to a description of the role of active conceptions of nonreward in interpretations of noncontinuous (partial) reinforcement effects.

[4] O. H. Mowrer, *Learning Theory and Behavior* (New York: John Wiley & Sons, 1960), 409.
[5] W. K. Estes, "The Statistical Approach to Learning Theory," in S. Koch (ed.), *Psychology: A Study of a Science,* Vol. 2 (New York: McGraw-Hill Book Company, 1959), 417.

Nonreward in Interpretations of Partial Reinforcement

In his 1958 chapter on learning, Lawrence differentiates between "intertrial" and "intratrial" interpretations of the Partial Reinforcement Effect (PRE)—the finding that partial or intermittent reinforcement in learning leads to greater resistance to extinction than does continuous reinforcement. Intertrial explanations attribute the PRE in one way or another to immediately carried-over traces of stimulation from one trial to the next in acquisition. According to such interpretations, it is on the basis of such traces that acquisition is more clearly discriminated from extinction by continuously than by partially reinforced subjects. Intratrial explanations ascribe the PRE to some kind of learned mechanism developing on each trial in acquisition and having its effect, associatively, later in extinction. There have been two classes of intertrial explanations. In both cases the classes can be termed Cognitive-Expectancy (C-E) interpretations, and Stimulus-Response (S-R) interpretations.

Generally speaking, the intertrial interpretations were an earlier development than the intratrial interpretations. Early C-E interpretations were the "common sense" expectancy hypothesis which emerged out of the early important experiments of Humphreys (e.g., 1939, 1940) and the discrimination hypothesis developed and tested by Bitterman and his associates (e.g., Bitterman, Fedderson, & Tyler, 1953). On the S-R side, the major intertrial explanation (apart from the "response unit" interpretation which applies to chained or highly massed responses but not to discrete trial learning) was the Hull-Sheffield hypothesis tested by Sheffield (1949). Weinstock's (1954) demonstration that partial reinforcement effects were not eliminated even when trials were separated by 24 hours, and an experiment by Wilson, Weiss, and Amsel (1955) disconfirming the earlier results of Sheffield helped to set the stage for, and indeed to provide, intratrial explanations of, the PRE. Much later, in fact very recently, there has been strong contraindication for a discrimination hypothesis in the work of Jenkins (1961) and of Theios (1962). Jenkins, using pigeons in a Skinner-type situation, and Theios, using rats in a runway, have found that the PRE is sustained when a large number of continuous reinforcements are interpolated between discrete trial partial reinforcement and extinction. This means that a large number of continuous reinforcements immediately before extinction and following partial reinforcement does not neutralize the partial reinforcement effect. Since the basis for discriminating acquisition from extinction is now the same for partially as for continuously reinforced subjects, and the PRE persists, an interpretation is required, as Theios indicates, in terms of "relatively permanent effects of nonreinforcement which can be sustained through blocks of continuous reinforcement."

Intratrial explanations of the PRE concern themselves in one way or another with processes following nonreward. Until recently, the intratrial explanations were the exclusive property of S-R psychologists. Weinstock's (1954) contiguity-interference hypothesis was perhaps the earlist of these, but was followed in short order by a variety of neo-Hullian hypotheses. All of these are what I would term conditioning expectancy hypotheses as opposed to cognitive-expectancy hypotheses of the PRE. All depend upon constructs of the anticipatory goal response type, representing responses which develop in strength within trials. There are three neo-Hullian interpretations of the PRE, all of which were first proposed to account for particular experimental findings. The first emerged out of a study by Wilson, Weiss, and Amsel (1955) and was subsequently elaborated and tested in some detail (Amsel, 1958). It attributes the PRE to the evocation of frustration by nonreward in partial reinforcement, to the conditioning of anticipatory frustration ($r_F - s_F$) to cues in the instrumental sequence, and to the association of s_F with approach responses in acquisition. Logan's interpretation of the PRE (Logan, Beier, & Kincaid, 1956) is that it depends on the extinction of r_G to "postreinforcement-time cues." Kendler and his associates (Kendler, Pliskoff, D'Amato, & Katz, 1957) have offered an interpretation similar to the one I have favored, except they choose a neutral designation of nonreward effects in acquisition and refer to anticipatory nonreward and not to anticipatory frustration. Spence (1960) has recently come out in favor of the same kind of interpretation and has employed the r_F construct to account for acquisition phenomena in partial reinforcement. Consequently, it seems safe to say that a prominent interpretation of the PRE in neo-Hullian writings is a conditioning-expectancy position which identifies fractional anticipatory frustration as well as fractional anticipatory reward. . . .

. . . The details of the S-R position which I favor have been presented elsewhere (Amsel, 1958) in the form of a sequence of hypotheses identified with four stages of practice in discrete trial partial reinforcement or in discrimination learning (the first three stages are essentially the same for both). A fifth hypothesis which applies to discrimination learning has been added, and this will be important for some data which follow. The essence of the position is outlined below in relation to an apparatus we have been using. It was designed to differentiate the immediate motivating (energizing) effects of frustration exemplified by the so-called Frustration Effect (FE) from fractional anticipatory frustration (r_F), which represents the inhibiting feature of frustration. The apparatus is essentially, two runways in series, either in a straight line (e.g., Amsel & Roussel, 1952) or in the form of an L (e.g., Amsel & Hancock, 1957). The apparatus has a start box (SB), a first runway (Runway 1), a first goal box (G1), a second runway (Runway 2), and a second goal box (G2) in successive arrangement. Reward and nonreward are manipulated in G1, and the apparatus permits a separation of the frustrated response and changes in running speed indicating r_F (measured in Runway 1), from the frustration motivated response and changes indicating the FE (measured in Runway 2).

The sequence of hypotheses in terms of five stages of practice is as follows:

1. In Stage 1, $r_R - s_R$ [6] is developing in Runway 1 with early rewards, and nonreward (in G1) has no particular effect, as measured by the FE in Runway 2.

2. After the development of $r_R - s_R$ for the Runway 1 response, nonrewards elicit frustration, measured by the FE in Runway 2. This is Stage 2.

[6] I employ the term $r_R - s_R$ in the same manner as it is used in an earlier development, and for the same reason: ". . . $r_G - s_G$ is a general term covering all types of antedating conditioned response. Separately, these might be designated $r_R - s_R$, fractional anticipatory reward; $r_P - s_P$, fractional anticipatory punishment, usually termed fear or anxiety; and $r_F - s_F$, fractional anticipatory frustration." (See Abram Amsel, "The Role of Frustrative Nonreward in Noncontinuous Reward Situations," *Psychological Bulletin*, 1958, **55**, 102.) The meaning of $r_R - s_R$ is, however, not different from $r_G - s_G$ as Spence (1960) uses it in a similar connection. All that is intended here is a clarification of terminology in light of the fact that goal events may be positive (such as to elicit approach) or negative (such as to elicit avoidance).

3. When nonrewards elicit frustration, the cues in Runway 1 previously evoking r_R now also begin to evoke r_F. In Stage 3 these antedating goal response tendencies are temporarily in competition.

4. Since r_R and r_F cannot be elicited separately by differential cues in partial reinforcement, as they can in the latter stages of discrimination learning, and since the temporary conflict in partial reward training is resolved in favor of running to the intermittently rewarding goal box, s_F becomes associated with the instrumental approach response in Stage 4 of partial reinforcement training, providing the mechanism for the partial reinforcement effect. When extinction is carried out, partially reinforced subjects have been trained to respond (approach in the presence of antedating, frustration-produced stimuli), whereas consistently reinforced subjects have not. In discrimination situations there is a basis for the differential elicitation of approach and avoidance by s_R and s_F respectively in Stage 4.

5. Following discrimination, when r_F consistently precedes nonreward, the FE following nonreward should grow weaker, since nonreward is defined as frustrating only in the presence of r_R.

I have been suggesting that in a very important area of the analysis of behavior, the explanation of persistence of behavior in the face of nonrewards attributable to partial reinforcement, the role of nonreward as an active process has emerged in both cognitive-expectancy and in S-R conditioning interpretations. It would certainly seem to me that this is an area where the clearer, better worked out S-R language and conceptualization might provide a handle for a more workable expectancy theory.

There is, in addition, the matter of a basic difference between the cognitive and S-R interpretations of the PRE: the former says nonreward increases attractiveness; the latter says nonreward decreases attractiveness. Both positions can account for the PRE; both positions can account for faster extinction following large rewards than following smaller rewards; both can account for faster extinction following many rewards than following fewer rewards. However, a cognitive theory such as Festinger proposes would have difficulty with a finding of Hulse (1958) which has recently been confirmed by Wagner (1961a). In Hulse's words: ". . . large as compared with small rewards produced greater resistance to extinction if partial reinforcement were used, but *less* resistance to extinction if continuous reinforcement were used. . . ." [7] In the cognitive language of Festinger this would have to mean that the subjects develop "some extra preference about something in the situation" (greater resistance to extinction) when rewards are *small and continuous;* and that they do not develop the extra preference, in fact quite the opposite, when rewards are *small and partial.* The result of Hulse and of Wagner is clearly in line with the S-R interpretation in terms of anticipatory responses: Extinction is *faster* following continuous rewards of large than of small magnitudes because of the greater FE in extinction and subsequent faster development of r_F. However, in partial reinforcement there is opportunity to elicit FE and to build r_F during acquision. Under these circumstances, the larger magnitude of reward permits the mechanism for the PRE—the connection of s_F to continued approach—to develop more strongly. Consequently extinction should be *slower* following partial rewards of large magnitude than following partial rewards of small magnitude.

I am claiming that the S-R conditioning analysis of nonreward effects has much to recommend it. The question is, How much? To break the question down: Does inclusion of the concepts r_R and r_F in the analysis of partial reinforcement and discrimination learning provide us with explanatory power which a more parsimonious approach-avoidance analysis (e.g., D'Amato & Jagoda, 1960; Nissen, 1950) does not? Does this type of analysis of nonreward effects provide predictive power which a cognitive treatment of nonreward (e.g., Festinger, 1961) does not?

My attempts to convince the reader that the answer to these last two questions is "yes" will take two forms: (a) Some data will be presented which bear on predictions already made on the basis of this type of analysis. I will claim that data such as these are not readily deducible from either a less specific cognitive language or from a more parsimonious approach-avoidance language. (b) I will offer an extention of frustrative nonreward theory designed to generate predictions about the course of discrimination learning following various prediscrimination experiences with partial and continuous reward.

Before proceeding to this extension of the theory of frustrative nonreward, a brief comment on the relation of the present position

[7] S. H. Hulse, Jr., "Amount and Percentage of Reinforcement and Duration of Goal Confinement in Conditioning and Extinction," *Journal of Experimental Psychology,* 1598, **56,** 56.

on nonreward to other theories of frustration. As I have indicated before (Amsel, 1958), ". . . we have been interested in certain active properties of nonreward following reward and no more than this is meant by the term *frustration* as we use it." [8] Nevertheless, the mechanism which has been outlined to explain the PRE, particularly the conditioning of r_F and the connection of s_F to continued approach as a result of intermittent reward, is certainly a candidate for the learning theory counterpart of "frustration tolerance" as employed in social psychology and psychopathology. The treatment of frustration from the viewpoint of theories of personality is beyond the scope of this paper; and there is no intent here to grapple with the multiple meanings the concept has in those contexts. However, it would seem possible to recast portions of the frustration theory of Rosenzweig (e.g., 1944) which deal with nonreward (failure or delay of "gratification") into the present terminology; and the treatment of frustration by Rotter (1954), as a discrepancy between reward expectancy and its occurrence, seems compatible with the mechanisms hypothesized here and with the theoretical extension I will propose.

*   *   *

EDITOR'S NOTE: Professor Amsel's paper concludes with a long section concerning the role of frustrative nonreward in discrimination learning. Most discrimination learning experiments begin with some prediscrimination training of Ss (so that they will respond in the discrimination situation itself) to one or both of the stimuli subsequently to be used in the discrimination study itself. Amsel identifies three aspects of prediscrimination training as crucial: (1) whether pretraining is to the stimulus which will be positive or the one which will be negative, or to both; (2) whether pretraining involves continuous or intermittent reinforcement; and (3) how many pretraining trials are given. A great many provocative predictions are made for the successive discrimination case (one stimulus presented on a given trial) from the combinations of these factors. To summarize Amsel's position briefly, he argues that condition (3) above interacts with condition (2) when pretraining is by intermittent reinforcement. In this case both anticipatory approach and anticipatory frustration (avoidance) are being developed. Early in training only anticipatory approach is developed. During an inter-

[8] Abram Amsel, "The Role of Frustrative Nonreward in Noncontinuous Reward Situations," *Psychological Bulletin,* 1958, **55,** 103.

mediate stage, anticipatory frustration also begins to develop, causing a conflict in approach and avoidance tendencies. If pretraining continues long enough, however, the anticipatory frustration stimuli become conditioned to the approach response itself. If pretraining is by continuous reinforcement, then the primary effect is to heighten the frustration effect occurring on nonrewarded trials during the discrimination problem itself.

Condition (1) above interacts with both of the other factors in that different methods of stimulus presentation affect the degree of generalization of both approach and avoidance tendencies to the stimuli when actually involved in the discrimination case. The different interactions of conditions (2) and (3) generalize differently according to the method of pretraining stimulus presentation.

Essentially, Amsel is taking the position that discrimination learning is a complex kind of approach-avoidance learning, with the avoidance component arising due to anticipatory frustration reactions. In other words, he continues his concept of an "active" role for nonreward, in contrast to the "passive" role given to it in some theories of discrimination learning.

There are some provocative predictions made in this section that are in the process of experimental testing in Professor Amsel's laboratory and elsewhere.

[8]
The Psychological Effects of
Insufficient Rewards
LEON FESTINGER

Some fields of psychology have for many years been dominated by ideas concerning the importance of rewards in the establishment and maintenance of behavior patterns. So dominant has this notion become that some of our most ingenious theoretical thinking has been devoted to imagining the existence of rewards in order to ex-

SOURCE: Leon Festinger, "The Psychological Effects of Insufficient Rewards," *American Psychologist*, 1961, **16**, 1–11. Reprinted by permission of the American Psychological Association and Leon Festinger.

plain behavior in situations where, plausibly, no rewards exist. It has been observed, for example, that under some circumstances an organism will persist in voluntarily engaging in behavior which is frustrating or painful. To account for such behavior it has, on occasion, been seriously proposed that the cessation of the frustration or pain is rewarding and thus reinforces the tendency to engage in the behavior.

I want to maintain that this type of explanation is not only unnecessary but also misleading. I certainly do *not* wish to say that rewards are unimportant, but I propose to show that the absence of reward or the existence of inadequate reward produces certain specific consequences which can account for a variety of phenomena which are difficult to deal with if we use our usual conceptions of the role of reward.

Before I proceed, I would like to say that most of the thinking and most of the experimental work which I will present are the result of collaboration between Douglas H. Lawrence and myself. Indeed, whatever you find interesting in what I say you may safely attribute primarily to him.

I will start my discussion in a rather roundabout manner with some remarks which concern themselves primarily with some aspects of the thinking processes of human beings. Human thinking is sometimes a strange mixture of "plausible" and "magical" processes. Let us examine more closely what I mean by this. For example, imagine that a person knows that some event is going to occur, and that the person can do something to prepare himself to cope more adequately with the impending event. Under such circumstances it is very reasonable (perhaps you might even want to use the word *rational*) for the person to do whatever is necessary in preparation for the coming event. Human thinking, however, also works in reverse. Consider a person who goes to a lot of trouble to prepare himself for a future event which might possibly occur. Such a person will subsequently tend to persuade himself that the event is rather likely to occur. There is nothing very plausible or rational about this kind of mental process—rather, it has almost a magical qaulity about it. . . .

. . . Consider some person who is strongly attracted to some goal. It is quite reasonable for this person to be willing to expend more effort, or to endure more pain, in order to reach the goal than he would be if he were less attracted. Once more, however, one finds the same process of reasoning in reverse. That is, if a person exerts a great deal of effort, or endures pain, in order to reach some ordinary objective, there is a strong tendency for him to persuade himself that the objective is especially valuable or especially desirable. An experiment conducted by Elliot Aronson and Judson Mills (1959) shows the effect quite nicely.

The subjects in the experiment by Aronson and Mills were college girls who volunteered to join small discussion groups. Each subject, when she appeared for the discussion group, was told that, instead of being put into a new group, she was being considered for inclusion in an ongoing group which had recently lost one of its members. However, the subject was told, because of the group's concern that the replacement be someone who would be able to discuss things freely and openly, the experimenter had agreed to test the replacement before admitting her to the group. Some subjects were then given a very brief and not painful test while others were given a rather extended and embarrassing test. The experimenter then, of course, told each subject that she had done well and was admitted to the group. Thus, there were some subjects who had attained membership in the group easily and some subjects who had endured a painful experience in order to be admitted to the group.

The experimenter then explained to the subject that the discussion was carried on by means of an intercommunication system, each girl being in a separate room. She was brought into her room which contained a microphone and earphones. The experimenter told her that the others had already started and perhaps it would be best for her not to participate in the discussion this time but just to listen. Next meeting, of course, she would participate fully. Speaking into the microphone the experimenter then went through the illusion of introducing her to the three other girls in the group. He then "disconnected" the microphone and gave the subject the earphones to wear. The subject then listened for about 25 minutes to a tape recording of a rather dull and halting discussion. All subjects, of course, heard exactly the same tape recording thinking they were listening to the actual live group discussion.

When the discussion was finished, the experimenter explained to the subject that, after each meeting, each of the girls filled out a "post-meeting reaction form." She was then given a questionnaire to complete which asked a variety of questions concerning how interesting she had found the discussion to be, how much she liked the other members of the group, and other similar questions. The results show, as anticipated, that those subjects who had gone through a painful procedure in order to be admitted to the group thought the discussion was more interesting and liked the other group members better than did those who had gained admission to the group easily. In other words, we see the same process operating here as we noted in the previous experiment. If someone is somehow induced to endure embarrassment in order to achieve something, she then persuades herself that what she has achieved is valuable.

In . . . the example which I have discussed (and one could present many more examples of similar nature) a situation has been produced where the organism has two pieces of information (or cognitions) which do not fit together. In the . . . example, the two cognitions which did not fit together were: (a) I have endured pain to attain an objective. (b) The objective is not very attractive. This kind of "nonfitting" relationship between two pieces of information may be termed a dissonant relation (Festinger, 1957). The reason, of course, that dissonance exists between these cognitions is that, psychologically, the obverse of one follows from the other. Psychologically, if an objective *is* very attractive, it follows that one would be willing to endure pain to attain it; or if the objective is *not* attractive, it follows that one does *not* endure pain to attain it. This specification of why a given relation between cognitions is dissonant also provides the clues to predicting specifically how the organism will react to the existence of the dissonance. Assuming that the organism will attempt to reduce the dissonance between the cognitions, there are obviously two major classes of ways in which this can be done. He can attempt to persuade himself that the pain which he endured was not really painful or he can attempt to persuade himself that the objective *is* very attractive.

I will not spend any more time than this in general theoretical discussion of the theory of dissonance and the reduction of dissonance. I hope that this small amount of general theoretical discussion will be enough to give context to the specific analysis of the psychological effects of insufficient rewards.

Let us consider in more detail what is suggested by the example of the experiment by Aronson and Mills and by the theory of cognitive dissonance. In that experiment the dissonance which was created was reduced by enhancing the value of the goal. This suggests that organisms may come to like and value things for which they have worked very hard or for which they have suffered. Looking at it from another aspect, one might say that they may come to value activities for which they have been inadequately rewarded. At first glance this may seem to contradict a widely accepted notion in psychology, namely, that organisms learn to like things for which they *have* been rewarded. In a sense it is contradictory, but not in the sense that it denies the operation of this widely assumed process. It does, however, state that another process also operates which is rather of an opposite character.

Let us analyze the situation with which we are concerned somewhat more carefully and more precisely. We are concerned with the dissonance between two possible cognitions. One of these is a cognition the organism has concerning his behavior, namely, I have voluntarily done something which, all other things being equal, I would avoid doing. The other is a cognition about the environment or about the result of his action, namely, the reward that has been obtained is inadequate. As we mentioned before, this dissonance can be reduced if the organism can persuade himself that he really likes the behavior in which he engaged or if he enhances for himself the value of what he has obtained as a result of his actions.

There is, of course, another way to reduce the dissonance, namely, for the organism to change his behavior. That is, having done something which resulted in an inadequate reward the organism can refuse to perform the action again. This means of reducing the dissonance is undoubtedly the one most frequently employed by organisms. If the organism obtains information which is dissonant with his behavior, he usually modifies his behavior so that it fits better what he knows concerning his environment. Here, however, I am going to consider only situations in which this means of reducing dissonance is not available to the organism. That is, I will consider only situations in which the organism is somehow tricked or seduced into continuing to engage in the activity in spite of the dissonance which is introduced. Under these circumstances we would expect one of the two previously mentioned dissonance reduction mechanisms to be used.

If one thinks for a while about the possible behavioral consequences of such a psychological process as we have described, an explanation suggests itself for the well-known finding that resistance to extinction is greater after partial reward than after complete reward. . . .

. . . Let us examine what occurs, psychologically, during a series of trials on which the behavior of an organism is only occasionally rewarded. Imagine a hungry animal who dashes frantically down some runway and into some so-called goal box only to find that there is nothing there. The cognition that he has obtained nothing is dissonant with the cognition that he has expended effort to reach the goal box. If this state of affairs were continually repeated, as we all know, the animal would reduce the dissonance by refusing to go to the goal box, that is, he would change his behavior. But, in a partial reward situation, the animal is tricked into continuing to run to the goal box because an appreciable number of times that he goes there he does find food. But, on each nonreward trial dissonance is introduced when the animal finds the goal box empty. The assumed process of dissonance reduction would lead us to expect that, gradually, the animal develops some extra preference either for the activity or for the goal box itself. A comparable animal that was rewarded every time he ran to the goal box would not develop any such extra preference.

Consider the situation, then, when extinction trials begin. In addition to realizing that food is no longer present, the partially rewarded animal also has to overcome his extra preference before he stops going to the goal box. We would thus expect "extinction" to take longer for a partially rewarded animal than for an animal that was always rewarded. The magnitude of the difference should be far greater than just the slight effect which would exist if the 100 per cent animal discovers more rapidly that the situation has changed.

If this explanation is correct, then the greater resistance to extinction following partial reward is a direct consequence of the process of dissonance reduction. This, of course, immediately suggests an extension of this line of reasoning to situations other than those involving partial reward. *Any* procedure which introduces dissonance during the training trials should similarly be expected to increase resistance to extinction since the same kind of dissonance reduction process should operate.

Let us, however, try to be precise about what kinds of procedures would introduce dissonance for an organism during training trials in an experiment. It is, fortunately, possible to define this operationally in a precise manner. Let us imagine that we test an organism in a single choice situation. In the case of a rat, for example, this might be simply an apparatus where, from the starting point the animal can turn either right or left. Let us further imagine that the organism we are testing is quite hungry and that, whichever alternative he chooses, he obtains food. We can, then, vary one at a time a variety of factors to discover what the organism will ordinarily avoid doing. One would, of course, find many such factors which would lead the organism not to choose the alternative with which that factor is associated. Dissonance will be created for the organism if he is somehow tricked into consistently engaging in an activity involving such a factor.

This may sound very involved so let me try to say it again, this time a bit less abstractly. Imagine that we test rats in a simple left-right choice apparatus and, no matter whether the animal goes left or right, he obtains food. But, imagine that if he goes left the animal must swim through water to get to the food, but if he goes right there is simply a short run down an alley to the food. Let us further imagine that, under such circumstances, the animal will consistently choose to go to the right, that is, he will avoid swimming through water. Armed with this knowledge concerning the behavior of the rat we can then assert the following: if one puts a rat in a situation where we somehow trick the rat into consistently swimming through water, dissonance will have been created.

Remembering what we have already said about the ways in which dissonance can be reduced in this kind of situation (provided that we are successful in tricking the organism into continuing to engage in the activity) we would then arrive at the following statement: any condition which the animal will avoid in the above-mentioned test situation will increase resistance to extinction in a nonchoice situation.

Let us look at some of the data which exist which are relevant to this statement. We know that if a hungry rat is put in a situation where he has a choice between a goal box where he is rewarded 100 per cent of the time and a goal box where he is rewarded only part of the time, he will fairly consistently go to the place where he is rewarded 100 per cent of the time. And, of course, we also know that where no choice is involved, partial reward increases resistance to extinction. But there are other variables or conditions which should increase resistance to extinction in a similar manner if our theoretical analysis is correct.

Consider the question of delay of reinforcement. Once more, thinking of our hypothetical test situation, we can be reasonably certain that a rat, if faced with a choice where one alternative led to immediate reward while the other alternative involved an appreciable delay before the rat was allowed to continue to the goal box to obtain food, the rat would rather consistently choose the alternative that led to immediate reward. We should then expect that, in a nonchoice situation, delay of reward should lead to greater resistance to extinction. Existing data show that this is indeed correct. Appreciable delay of reward does lead to greater resistance to extinction. I will briefly review some of the data which exist on delay of reward to give you some idea of the effect which is obtained.

The usual experiment that has been done on extinction following delay of reinforcement compares one condition in which the rats encounter no enforced delay between starting down a runway and obtaining food in the goal box with other conditions in which, on some trials, the rats are detained in a delay chamber before being allowed to proceed to the food. The usual period of delay which has been used has been about 30 seconds. Crum, Brown, and Bitterman (1951) and Scott and Wike (1956) both find that a group of rats delayed on half the trials shows much greater resistance to extinction than a group which was never delayed. In another experiment, Wike and McNamara (1957) ran three groups which differed in the percentage (and, of course, number) of trials on which they were delayed. They find that the larger the percentage or number of trials on which the animal experiences delay, the greater is the resistance to extinction. The same kind of result is obtained by Fehrer (1956), who compared rats who were delayed for 20 seconds on *every* trial with ones who were never delayed. She also finds that delay results in increased resistance to extinction.

Before we proceed to other matters, I would like to briefly raise a question concerning one kind of explanation that has frequently, in one form or another, been offered to account for increased resistance to extinction after partial reward. The basis of this kind of explanation, whether it be in terms of expectancy, or conditioning of cues, or any of a number of other varieties, rests in pointing out that there is more similarity between acquisition and extinction for partial reward conditions than for 100-per-cent reward conditions.

I would like to point out that this type of explanation is clearly not very useful in explaining the increased resistance to extinction after delay of reward. From the point of view of the explanation I am here proposing, however, partial reward and delay of reward clearly involve the same psychological processes.

Let us go on now to examine the matter of work and effort. I am sure it is fairly obvious to all of you now what I want to say about work and effort. If we return to a consideration of our hypothetical test situation we know that, given a choice between an effortless path to food and a path requiring expenditure of effort, the hungry animal will choose the effortless path rather regularly. Hence, in accordance with our analysis concerning dissonance and dissonance reduction, we would expect the requirement of greater effort during acquisition to lead to increased resistance to extinction.

It is surprising that, in spite of the relative consistency of results among the studies which exist in the literature, the effect of effort during acquisition on resistance to extinction has not been generally noted. People have rather tended to note the finding that the greater the effort required during extinction, the faster does extinction occur. But the data are also clear with respect to the effect of effort during acquisition. They show quite clearly that, holding effort during extinction constant, the more effort required during acquisition, the more resistance there is to extinction. The data from one of the more adequately controlled experiments will suffice to illustrate the effect.

Aiken (1957) reports an experiment in which the animal was required to press a panel in order to gain access to food. Some rats were required to exert little effort while others were required to exert considerable effort during training. Half of the animals in each condition were extinguished with the low effort requirement and half with the high effort requirement. Holding effort during extinction constant, the results show clearly that the average number of trials to a criterion of extinction was considerably greater for the high effort acquisition condition than for the low effort acquisition condition. Other experiments in the literature also show this same effect if one examines the data carefully. It should once more be pointed out that any explanation of this effect which depends upon a notion of similarity between acquisition and extinction conditions is clearly inadequate.

One could list many other specific conditions which, analyzed in the same way, would be expected to increase resistance to extinction. I have chosen the three preceding ones to discuss because reasonably good data concerning them exist in the literature. Now, however, I would like to return to a more thorough consideration of the partial reward situation.

I have stated that, on nonrewarded trials in a partial reward situation, dissonance is introduced into the animal's cognition when he realizes that there is no food available. The amount of dissonance can, of course, vary in magnitude. It is important for us to consider the operational variables which will affect the total magnitude of dissonance which is introduced in this manner. This total magnitude of dissonance, of course, will determine how much dissonance reduction occurs through the development of extra preferences (always assuming that the animal does not change his behavior) and hence will determine the resistance to extinction.

In the past, it has generally been assumed that the major operational variable affecting resistance to extinction is the ratio of reward. That is, the smaller the proportion of rewarded trials, the greater the resistance to extinction. However, one might reason that since dissonance is created for the animal on every nonrewarded trial, it seems plausible to suppose that the major operational variable which will affect the resistance to extinction is, rather, the sheer total number of nonrewarded trials which the animal has experienced rather than the ratio of nonreward. From the data in published experiments it is impossible to assess whether or not this is correct since these two variables are completely confounded in the literature. Experiments on partial reward have always held constant either the number of rewarded trials or else the total number of trials that the animal experiences. It is clear, of course, that when either of these quantities is held constant, the number of nonrewarded trials is perfectly correlated with the ratio of nonreward and so the effects cannot be separated.

It is possible, perhaps, to get some hunch about this, however, from examining the results of experiments which have used rather few training trials. If we are correct, these experiments should show very weak effects of partial reward on resistance to extinction. Sheffield (1949), for example, using a total of 30 trials (only 15 nonrewarded trials) found very small differences between extinction after partial and complete reward. Wilson, Weiss, and Amsel (1955) and also Lewis (1956), replicating the Sheffield experiment almost exactly, also find such small differences that it requires an analysis of covariance to make them appear significant. However, Weinstock (1954), using a similar apparatus, but employing 75 training trials, finds huge and unmistakable differences.

It is unnecessary to belabor the matter by quoting many studies here since it is all a matter of hunch and impression. In general, when one goes through the literature one gets the impression that the experiments which show small effects after partial reward have tended to employ rather few trials. But comparison of this kind between different experiments done by different experimenters is a very shabby business at best since the variation from experimenter to experimenter can be quite large for unknown reasons. The question seemed important enough, however, so that Lawrence and I thought it worthwhile to do a study which could answer the question. The study was carried out through the kind efforts of John Theios. I would like to describe it to you briefly.

The general design of the study is very simple and does not differ in any essential way from the usual study which has been done on the effects of partial reward. The major difference was that we were primarily concerned with seeing the effects of the absolute number of nonrewarded trials and with being able to separate these effects from the effects of ratio of reward. We employed four different conditions of "number of unrewarded trials." Some groups experienced 0 unrewarded trials; some groups of animals experienced a total of 16 unrewarded trials in the apparatus; still other groups experienced a moderate number of unrewarded trials, namely, 27; and finally some groups were run who experience very many unrewarded trials, namely, 72.

Within these conditions, by varying the total number of trials, different conditions of ratio of reward were set up. Some animals were run with 33 per cent reward, others with 50 per cent reward, and still others with 67 per cent reward. Of course, it was not possible to vary the ratio of reward for animals in the condition of 0 unrewarded trials but the animals were run for varying numbers of trials anyhow. . . . During preliminary training, of course, all groups were rewarded 100 per cent of the time. There were between 11 and 16 animals in each condition. It will be noted that we did not run a condition of 67 per cent reward and 27 unrewarded trials. The reason for this is simple. We ran out of patience and decided this condition was not essential.

It will also be noted that three groups of 0 unrewarded trials were run so that the total number of trials brackets the entire range for the other groups.

Figure 1 shows the results of the experiment. Along the horizontal axis of the figure are indicated the various values of number of unrewarded trials which we employed and along the ordinate are the average number of trials to reach a criterion of extinction. Each

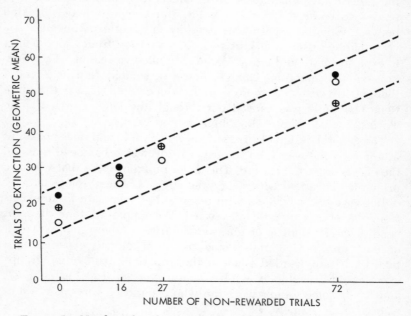

FIGURE 1. Number of trials to extinction after partial reward.

circle on the figure represents the results for one of our experimental conditions. The empty circles represent the data for those with the fewest total number of trials. Thus, except for the 0 unrewarded trials conditions, these empty circles represent the data for the 33 per cent reward conditions. Similarly, the dark circles represent the longest number of total trials and hence, for the partial reward groups, represent the 67 per cent reward conditions.

It is clear from an examination of the figure that, holding constant the number of unrewarded trials, there were only slight differences among the different conditions of ratio of reward. On the other hand, the variable of total number of unrewarded trials has a large and significant effect. It would, indeed, seem that in these data the only variable affecting resistance to extinction after partial reward is the number of unrewarded trials. The results of the experiment are, hence, quite consistent with the interpretations which we have made from the theory of dissonance.

These data are, of course, encouraging but certainly not conclusive. It would be nice to be able to have more direct evidence that nonreward tends to result in the development of extra preferences. From the point of view of obtaining such more direct evidence concerning the validity of our theoretical interpretation, the partial reward situation is not very adequate. For one thing, our theoretical analysis states that quite different processes occur, psychologically, on rewarded and on unrewarded trials. In a partial reward situation, however, the animal experiences both kinds of trials and, hence, an attempt to separate the effects of the two kinds of trials is bound to be indirect. And, of course, the possibility always exists that the increased resistance to extinction may depend upon some more or less complicated interaction between rewarded and unrewarded trials.

It would then be desirable to be able to compare pure conditions of reward and nonreward. That is, we could test the theory more adequately if we could compare the resistance to extinction of two groups of animals, one of which had always been rewarded in a given place, and the other of which had *never* been rewarded in that same place. This, of course, presents technical problems of how one manages to induce an animal to consistently go to a place where he never gets rewarded. This problem, however, can be solved by employing a variation of what is, essentially, a delay of reward experiment. With the very able assistance and hard work of Edward Uyeno we proceeded to do a series of such experiments in an attempt to get more direct validation of our theoretical derivations. I would like to describe some of these experiments for you.

The apparatus we used was a runway with two boxes in addition to the starting box. The two boxes were, of course, quite easily distinguishable. We will refer to one of them as the end-box and to the other as the mid-box. From the starting place, the animal was to run through a section of alley to the mid-box and then through another section of alley to the end-box. One group of rats was fed on every trial in the mid-box and also fed on every trial in the end-box. We will refer to this group as the 100-per-cent reward condition. Another group of rats was never fed in the mid-box but, instead, was delayed there for the same amount of time that it took the other to eat its food. These animals then continued to the end-box where they were also fed on every trial. We will refer to this group as the 0-per-cent reward condition. The designations of 100-per-cent and 0-per-cent reward refer, of course, to the reward in the mid-box. Both groups were rewarded on every trial in the end-box and this, of course, is what induced the animals in the 0-per-cent reward condition to run consistently to a place where they were never rewarded.

The procedure which was employed in extinction was also somewhat different from the usual procedure in a delay of reward experiment. Because we were interested in comparing the two groups of animals in their willingness to go to the mid-box where one group had always, and the other group had never, been fed, we ran extinction trials only from the starting position to the mid-box. During extinction, of course, no food was present for either condition and after a short period of time in the mid-box the animals were returned to their home cage. Thus, from this experiment we have a better comparison of the effects of reward and of nonreward. Figure 2 shows the average running times for the two groups during extinction.

The figure shows the data for the first 30 extinction trials averaged in groups of 3 trials each. It is clear from the figure that there is a very marked difference between the two groups of animals. Those who were always fed in the mid-box start off running quite fast (reflecting their speed of running during acquisition) but slow down very rapidly. Those animals that were never fed in the mid-box start off more slowly (again reflecting their speed of running during acquisition) but they do not show as rapid a rate of extinction. Indeed, between the fourth and fifth blocks of trials the two curves cross over and thereafter the animals run considerably faster to a place where they have never been rewarded than they do to a place where they have always been rewarded.

One may certainly conclude from these data that increased resistance to extinction results from nonreward and that an explanation of the partial reward effect in terms of some interaction between reward and nonreward is not very tenable. Actually, in the experiment I have just described we ran a third group of animals which was rewarded 50 per cent of the time in the mid-box and the results for these animals during extinction fall nicely midway between the two curves in Figure 2. The resistance to extinction of those who were never fed in the mid-box is greater than that of either of the other two groups of animals.

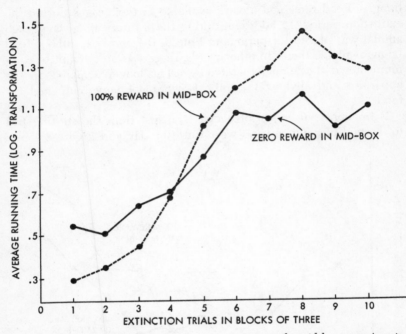

FIGURE 2. Running time during extinction in single mid-box experiment.

At the risk of being terribly repetitious, I would like to remind you at this point of the explanation I am offering for these data. Briefly, dissonance is introduced as a result of the insufficient reward or absence of reward. As long as the organism is prevented from changing his behavior, the dissonance tends to be reduced by developing some extra preference about something in the situation. The existence of this extra preference leads to the stronger inclination to continue running during extinction trials.

If this explanation is correct, however, one should be able to observe the effects of this extra preference even in a situation where all the motivation for food was removed. Indeed, it would seem that this would be a better test of this theoretical explanation. We consequently repeated the experiment I have just described to you with one modification. Three days were allowed to elapse between the end of acquisition and the beginning of extinction. During these 3 days food was always present in the cages so that by the time the extinction trials started the animals were quite well fed and not hungry. Food remained always available in their cages during the extinction period. In addition, during the 3 intervening days, each animal was placed for periods of time in the end-box without food being available there. In other words, there was an attempt to communicate to the animal that food was no longer available in the apparatus and anyhow the animals were not very motivated for food.

Extinction trials were, of course, run just from the starting box to the mid-box. Three trials were run each day and Figure 3 shows

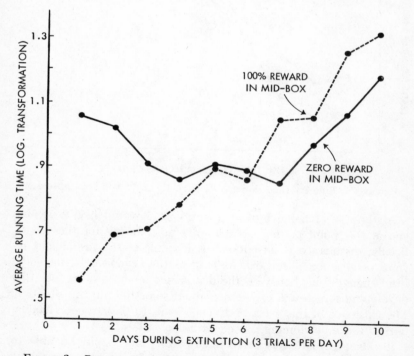

FIGURE 3.   Running time while satiated during extinction in single mid-box experiment.

the results for the first 10 days of extinction. It is clear from an examination of the figure that the results are very similar to the previous results and are, in a sense, even stronger. Those animals who were always fed in the mid-box start off relatively fast and as extinction trials progress the curve shows steady and rather rapid increase in running time. In short, one obtains a familiar kind of extinction curve for these animals.

The group that was never fed in the mid-box, however, shows a very different pattern of behavior. They start off much more slowly than the other group but, for the first 4 days of extinction, they actually run faster than at the beginning. By the seventh day the two curves have crossed and thereafter the 0-per-cent reward group runs faster than the 100-per-cent reward group. It is also interesting to note that, for the 0-per-cent reward group, through the eighth day, one can see no evidence of any extinction having occurred at all. If one is inclined to do so, one can certainly see in these data some evidence that an extra preference of rather weak strength exists for the animals that were never rewarded in the mid-box.

We were sufficiently encouraged by these results so that we proceeded to perform what I, at least, regarded as a rather ambitious experiment. Before I describe the experiment, let me briefly explain the reasoning which lay behind it. It is plausible to suppose that the extra preference which the organism develops in order to reduce dissonance may be focused on any of a variety of things. Let me explain this by using the experiment I have just described as an illustration. Those animals who were never fed in the mid-box, and thus experienced dissonance, could have developed a liking for the activity of running down the alley to the mid-box, they could have developed a preference for some aspect of the mid-box itself, or they could have developed a preference for any of the things they did or encountered subsequent to leaving the mid-box. Experimentally, of course, there was no control over this.

It occurred to us, in thinking about this, that if the dissonance were reduced, at least to some extent, by developing a preference for something about the *place* where the dissonance was introduced, then it would be possible to show the same effects in a very well controlled experiment. In other words, if the dissonance introduced by absence of reward were reduced, at least in part, by developing some liking for the place where they were not rewarded, then one could compare two groups of animals, both of which experienced the identical amount of dissonance, but who would be expected to develop preferences for different places.

To do this we used the same basic technique as in the previous two experiments I have described but with an important modification. Instead of one mid-box, two mid-boxes were used. From the starting box the animals went to Mid-box A, from there to Mid-box B, and from there to the end-box where all animals received food on every trial. Two groups of animals were run in this experiment. Group A was delayed in Mid-box A for a period of time and then was allowed to run directly through Mid-box B to the end-box. Group B was allowed to run directly through Mid-box A but was delayed for a period of time in Mid-box B before being allowed to go to the end-box. In other words, both groups of animals had identical experience. The only difference between the groups lay in the particular box in which they were delayed. (All three boxes were, of course, quite distinctive.) For the extinction trials the animals were satiated as in the preceding experiment. For the extinction trials, the animals were run only from Box A to Box B. That is, during extinction the animals were placed directly into Box A, the door was then opened, and when they ran to Box B were removed to their home cage.

Thus, Group A during extinction was running away from the place where they had been delayed, while Group B was running to the place where they had been delayed. If some extra preference had developed for the place where they had been delayed, we would expect Group B to show more resistance to extinction than Group A. In short, during extinction, Group B should behave like the 0-per-cent reward groups in the previous experiments. Group A, however, should behave during extinction more like the 100-per-cent reward animals in the preceding experiments.

Figure 4 shows the data for these two groups of animals for the first 10 days of extinction, three trials having been run on each day. The two curves in the figure must, by now, look very familiar to you. The same result is obtained as in the two previous experiments. The initial difference between the two groups again reflects their previous running speed in that section of the apparatus. During acquisition, Group B ran more hesitantly in the section between the two mid-boxes than did Group A. This difference, of course, still exists at the start of the extinction trials. Thereafter, however, Group A, which was running away from its delay box, rapidly increases its running time. Group B, which was running to its delay box, does not increase its time at all and shows no evidence of any extinction during 30 trials. By the fourth day of extinction, the two curves have crossed and thereafter Group B consistenly runs faster than Group A.

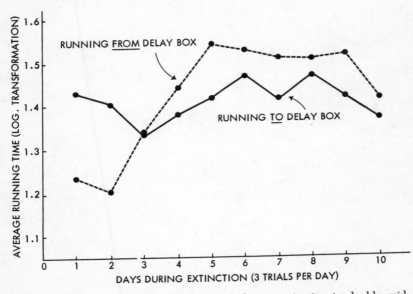

FIGURE 4. Running time while satiated during extinction in double mid-box experiment.

If one looks carefully at all the data, I think one finds reasonable evidence that insufficient reward does lead to the development of extra preference. This extra preference, at least in the white rat, seems to be of a rather mild nature, but the magnitude of the effect is quite sufficient to account for the increased resistance to extinction after partial reward or after delay of reward.

Let us then briefly examine the implications of these findings and of the theory of dissonance for our traditional conception of how reward functions. It seems clear that the inclination to engage in behavior after extrinsic rewards are removed is not so much a function of past rewards themselves. Rather, and paradoxically, such persistence in behavior is increased by a history of nonrewards or inadequate rewards. I sometimes like to summarize all this by saying that rats and people come to love things for which they have suffered.

Bibliography

Adelman, H. M., & Maatsch, J. L. Resistance to extinction as a function of the type of response elicited by frustration. *J. exp. Psychol.*, 1955, **50**, 61–65.

Adelman, H. M., & Rosenbaum, G. Extinction of instrumental behavior as a function of frustration at various distances from the goal. *J. exp. Psychol.*, 1954, **47**, 429–432.

Aiken, E. G. The effort variable in the acquisition, extinction, and spontaneous recovery of an instrumental response. *J. exp. Psychol.*, 1957, **53**, 47–51.

Allport, G. W., Bruner, J. S., & Jandorf, E. M. Personality and social catastrophe. In C. Kluckhohn & H. A. Murray (Ed.), *Personality in nature, society and culture*. New York: Knopf, 1949.

Amsel, A. Fractional anticipatory frustration: a suggested addition to Hull's inhibition theory. Paper read at Sth. Soc. for Phil. and Psychol. Roanoke, Va., March, 1951.

Amsel, A. The role of frustrative nonreward in noncontinuous reward situations. *Psychol. Bull.*, 1958, **55**, 102–119.

Amsel, A. Frustrative Nonreward in Partial Reinforcement and Discrimination Learning: Some Recent History and a Theoretical Extension. *Psychol. Rev.*, 1962, **69**, 306–328.

Amsel, A., Ernhart, C. B., & Galbrecht, C. R. Magnitude of frustration effect and strength of antedating goal factors. *Psychol. Rep.*, 1961, **8**, 183–186.

Amsel, A., & Hancock, W. Motivational properties of frustration: III. Relation of frustration effect to antedating goal factors. *J. exp. Psychol.*, 1957, **53**, 126–131.

Amsel, A., & Penick, E. The influence of early experience on the frustration effect. *J. exp. Psychol.*, 1962, **63**, 167–176.

Amsel, A., & Prouty, D. L. Frustrative factors in selective learning with reward and nonreward as discriminanda. *J. exp. Psychol.*, 1959, **57**, 224–230.

Amsel, A., & Roussel, J. Motivational properties of frustration: I. Effect on a running response of the addition of frustration to the motivational complex. *J. exp. Psychol.*, 1952, **43**, 363–368.

Amsel, A., & Ward, J. S. Motivational properties of frustration: II. Frustration drive stimulus and frustration reduction in selective learning. *J. exp. Psychol.*, 1954, **48**, 37–47.

Armus, H. L. Effect of magnitude of reinforcement on acquisition and extinction of a running response. *J. exp. Psychol.*, 1959, **58**, 61–63.

Aronson, E., & Mills, J. The effect of severity of initiation on liking for a group. *J. abnorm. soc. Psychol.*, 1959, **59**, 177–181.

Azrin, N. H. Time-out from positive reinforcement. *Science*, 1961, **133**, 382–383.

Barker, R. G. Frustration as an experimental problem: V. The effect of frustration upon cognitive ability. *Charact. & Pers.*, 1938, **7**, 145–150.

Barker, R., Dembo, T., & Lewin, K. Frustration and regression: an experiment with young children. *Univ. Iowa Stud. Child Welf.*, 1941, **18**, No. 1.

Beach, F. A., & Jaynes, J. Effects of early experience upon the behavior of animals. *Psychol. Bull.*, 1954, **51**, 239–263.

Bergmann, G. The logic of psychological concepts. *Phil. Sci.*, 1951, **18**, 93–110.

Bergmann, G., & Spence, K. W. Operationism and theory in psychology. *Psychol. Rev.*, 1941, **48**, 1–14.

Berkowitz, L. Repeated frustrations and expectations in hostility arousal. *J. abnorm. soc. Psychol.*, 1960, **60**, 422–429.

Berkowitz, L. *Aggression: a social psychological analysis.* New York: McGraw-Hill, 1962.

Bindra, D. *Motivation: a systematic reinterpretation.* New York: Ronald, 1959.

Birch, D. Discrimination learning as a function of the ratio of nonreinforced to reinforced trials. *J. comp. physiol. Psychol.*, 1955, **55**, 456–464.

Bitterman, M. E., Feddersen, W. E., & Tyler, D. W. Secondary reinforcement and the discrimination hypothesis. *Amer. J. Psychol.*, 1953, **66**, 456–464.

Block, Jeanne, & Martin, B. Predicting the behavior of children under frustration. *J. abnorm. soc. Psychol.*, 1955, **51**, 281–285.

Boring, E. G. *The physical dimensions of consciousness.* New York: Appleton-Century-Crofts, 1933.

Bower, G. H. A contrast effect in differential conditioning. *J. exp. Psychol.*, 1961, **63**, 196–199.

Bower, G. H., & Stocks, D. Graded frustration effect as a function of graded reduction in reward. Paper read at Psychonomic Soc., Chicago, 1960.

Brown, J. S., & Farber, I. E. Emotions conceptualized as intervening variables—with suggestions toward a theory of frustration. *Psychol. Bull.*, 1951, **48**, 465–495.

Bush, R. R., & Mosteller, F. A mathematical model for simple learning. *Psychol. Rev.,* 1951, **58**, 313–323.

Cantor, G. N., & Spiker, C. C. Effects of nonreinforced trials on discrimination learning in preschool children. *J. exp. Psychol.,* 1954, **47**, 256–258.

Cantania, A. C. Behavioral contrast in a multiple and concurrent schedule of reinforcement. *J. exp. anal. Behav.,* 1961, **4**, 335–342.

Child, I. L., & Waterhouse, I. K. Frustration and the quality of performance: I. A critique of the Barker, Dembo, and Lewin experiment. *Psychol. Rev.,* 1952, **59**, 351–362.

Child, I. L., & Waterhouse, I. K. Frustration and the quality of performance: II. A theoretical statement. *Psychol. Rev.,* 1953, **60**, 127–139.

Crandall, V. J. Induced frustration and punishment-reward expectancy in thematic apperception stories. *J. consult. Psychol.,* 1951, **15**, 400–404.

Crespi, L. P. Amount of reinforcement and level of performance. *Psychol. Rev.,* 1944, **51**, 341–357.

Crum, J., Brown, W. L., & Bitterman, M. E. The effect of partial and delayed reinforcement on resistance to extinction. *Amer. J. Psychol.,* 1951, **74**, 228–237.

D'Amato, M. R., & Jagoda, H. Effects of extinction trials on discrimination reversal. *J. exp. Psychol.,* 1960, **59**, 254–260.

Davitz, J. R. The effects of previous training on postfrustration behavior. *J. abnorm. soc. Psychol.,* 1952, **47**, 309–315.

Denny, M. R., & Dunham, M. D. The effect of differential nonreinforcement of the incorrect response on the learning of the correct response in the simple T-maze. *J. exp. Psychol.,* 1951, **41**, 382–389.

Dewey, J. *How we think.* Boston: Heath, 1910.

Dollard, J., Doob, L. W., Miller, N. E., Mowrer, O. H., & Sears, R. R. *Frustration and aggression.* New Haven: Yale Univ. Press, 1939.

Duffy, Elizabeth. Emotion: an example of the need for reorientation in psychology. *Psychol. Rev.,* 1934, **41**, 184–198.

Duffy, Elizabeth. Leeper's "motivational theory of emotion." *Psychol. Rev.,* 1948, **55**, 324–328.

Eninger, M. U. The role of generalized approach and avoidance tendencies in brightness discrimination. *J. comp. physiol. Psychol.,* 1953, **40**, 398–402.

Estes, W. K. Toward a statistical theory of learning. *Psychol. Rev.,* 1950, **57**, 94–107.

Estes, W. K. The statistical approach to learning theory. In S. Koch (Ed.), *Psychology: a study of a science,* Vol. 2. New York: McGraw-Hill, 1959.

Farber, I. E. Response fixation under anxiety and non-anxiety conditions. *J. exp. Psychol.,* 1948, **38**, 111–131.

Fehrer, E. Effects of amount of reinforcement and of pre- and post-reinforcement delays on learning and extinction. *J. exp. Psychol.*, 1956, **52**, 167–176.

Feldman, R. S. The specificity of the fixated response in the rat. *J. comp. physiol. Psychol.*, 1953, **46**, 487–492.

Ferster, C. B. Withdrawal of positive reinforcement as punishment. *Science*, 1957, **126**, 509.

Ferster, C. B. Control of behavior in chimpanzees and pigeons by time out from positive reinforcement. *Psychol. Monogr.*, 1958, **72**, 8, (Whole No. 461).

Ferster, C. B., & Skinner, B. F. *Schedules of reinforcement.* New York: Appleton-Century-Crofts, 1957.

Festinger, L. *A theory of cognitive dissonance.* Stanford, Calif.: Stanford Univ. Press, 1957.

Festinger, L. The psychological effects of insufficient rewards. *Amer. Psychologist*, 1961, **16**, 1–11.

Finch, G. Chimpanzee frustration responses. *Psychosom. Med.*, 1942, **4**, 233–251.

Fitzwater, M. E. The relative effect of reinforcement and nonreinforcement in establishing a form discrimination. *J. comp. physiol. Psychol.*, 1952, **45**, 476–481.

Frank, L. K. Time perspective. *J. soc. Phil.*, 1939, **4**, 293–312.

French, J. R. P., Jr. Organized and unorganized groups under fear and frustration. Authority and frustration: studies in topological and vector psychology III. *Univ. Iowa Stud. Child Welf.*, 1944, **20**, 231–307.

Geier, F. M., & Tolman, E. C. Goal distance and restless activity: I. The goal gradient of restless activity. *J. comp. Psychol.*, 1943, **35**, 197–204.

Goodrich, K. P. Performance in different segments of an instrumental response chain as a function of reinforcement schedule. *J. exp. Psychol.*, 1959, **57**, 57–63.

Grice, G. R., & Goldman, H. M., Generalized extinction and secondary reinforcement in visual discrimination learning with delayed reward. *J. exp. Psychol.*, 1955, **50**, 197–200.

Grosslight, J. H., & Child, I. L. Persistence as a function of previous experience of failure followed by success. *Amer. J. Psychol.*, 1947, **60**, 378–387.

Grove, G. R., & Eninger, M. U. The relative importance of approach and avoidance tendencies in brightness discrimination learning. Paper read at Midwest. Psychol. Ass., Chicago, 1952.

Haggard, D. F. Acquisition of a simple running response as a function of partial and continuous schedules of reinforcement. *Psychol. Rec.*, 1959, **9**, 11–18.

Hamilton, G. V. *An introduction to objective psychopathy.* St. Louis: Mosby, 1925.

Harlow, H. F., & Hicks, L. H. Discrimination learning theory: Uniprocess vs. duoprocess. *Psychol. Rev.*, 1957, **64**, 104–109.

Haslerud, G. M. Some interrelations of behavioral measures of frustration in chimpanzees. (III) *Charact. & Pers.*, 1938–39, **7**, 137–139.

Hilgard, E. R. Experimental approaches to psychoanalysis. In E. Pumpian-Mindlin (Ed.), *Psychoanalysis as science*. Stanford, Calif.: Stanford Univ. Press, 1952.

Hollenberg, E., & Sperry, M. Some antecedents of aggression and effects of frustration in doll play. *Personality*, 1951, **1**, 32–43.

Holz, W. C., & Azrin, N. H. Discriminative properties of punishment. *J. exp. anal. Behav.*, 1961, **4**, 225–232.

Hull, C. L. The concept of the habit-family hierarchy, and maze learning: Parts I & II. *Psychol. Rev.*, 1934, **41**, 33–54; 134–152.

Hull, C. L. The problem of intervening variables in molar behavior theory. *Psychol. Rev.*, 1943, **50**, 273–291. (a)

Hull, C. L. *Principles of behavior*. New York: Appleton-Century-Crofts, 1943. (b)

Hull, C. L. *A behavior system*. New Haven: Yale University Press, 1952.

Hull, C. L., Livingston, J. R., Rouse, R. O., & Barker, A. N. True, sham, and esophageal feeding as reinforcements. *J. comp. physiol. Psychol.*, 1951, **44**, 236–245.

Hulse, S. H., Jr. Amount and percentage of reinforcement and duration of goal confinement in conditioning and extinction. *J. exp. Psychol.*, 1958, **56**, 48–57.

Humphreys, L. G. The effect of random alternation of reinforcements on the acquisition and extinction of conditioned eyelid reactions. *J. exp. Psychol.*, 1939, **25**, 141–158.

Humphreys, L. G. Extinction of conditioned psychogalvanic response following two conditions of reinforcement. *J. exp. Psychol.*, 1940, **27**, 71–76.

Jenkins, H. M. Resistance to extinction when partial reinforcement is followed by various amounts of regular reinforcement. Paper read at Psychonomic Soc., New York, 1961.

Jenkins, R. L. Adaptive and maladaptive delinquency. *Nerv. Child*, 1955, **11**, 9–11.

Jenkins, W. O., & Stanley, J. C., Jr. Partial reinforcement: a review and critique. *Psychol. Bull.*, 1950, **47**, 193–234.

Keister, M. E., & Updegraff, R. A study of children's reactions to failure and an experimental attempt to modify them. *Child Develpm.*, 1937, **8**, 241–248.

Kendler, H. H., Pliskoff, S. S., D'Amato, M. R., & Katz, S. Nonreinforcements versus reinforcements as variables in the partial reinforcement effect. *J. exp. Psychol.*, 1957, **53**, 269–276.

Kleemeier, R. W. Fixation and regression in the rat. *Psychol. Monogr.*, 1942, **54**, 1–34.

Köhler, W. *Gestalt psychology.* New York: Liveright, 1929.

Krech, D. Notes toward a psychological theory. *J. Pers.*, 1949, **19**, 66–87.

Lachman, R. The influence of thirst and schedules of reinforcement–non-reinforcement ratios upon brightness discrimination. *J. exp. Psychol.*, 1961, **62**, 80–87.

Lambert, W. W., & Solomon, R. L. Extinction of a running response as a function of distance of block point from the goal. *J. comp. physiol. Psychol.*, 1952, **45**, 269–279.

Lawrence, D. H., & Festinger, L. *Deterrents and reinforcement: the psychology of insufficient reward.* Stanford, Calif.: Stanford Univ. Press, 1962.

Lawson, R. *Learning and behavior.* New York: Macmillan, 1960.

Lawson, R., & Marx, M. H. Frustration: theory and experiment. *Genet. psychol. Monogr.*, 1958, **57**, 393–464. (a)

Lawson, R., & Marx, M. H. A comparison of some presumed frustrating and secondary-reinforcing operations. *J. comp. physiol. Psychol.*, 1958, **51**, 742–746. (b)

Leeper, R. W. A motivational theory of emotion to replace "emotion as disorganized response." *Psychol. Rev.*, 1948, **55**, 5–21.

Levy, D. M. Experiments on the sucking reflex and social behavior of dogs. *Amer. J. Orthopsychiat.*, 1934, **4**, 203–224.

Levy, D. M. On instinct-satiation: an experiment on the pecking behavior of chickens. *J. gen. Psychol.*, 1938, **18**, 327–348.

Lewin, K. *A dynamic theory of personality.* New York: McGraw-Hill, 1935.

Lewin, K. *Principles of topological psychology.* New York: McGraw-Hill, 1936.

Lewin, K. The conceptual representation and measurement of psychological force. *Duke Univ. Series Contr. Psychol. Theory*, 1938, 1, No. 4.

Lewis, D. J. Acquisition, extinction, and spontaneous recovery as a function of percentage of reinforcement and intertrial intervals. *J. exp. Psychol.*, 1956, **51**, 45–53.

Logan, F. A., Beier, E. M., & Kincaid, W. D. Extinction following partial and varied reinforcement. *J. exp. Psychol.*, 1956, **52**, 65–70.

Longstreth, L. E. The relationship between expectations and frustrations in children. *Child Develpm.*, 1960, **31**, 667–671.

MacCorquodale, K., & Meehl, P. E. On a distinction between hypothetical constructs and intervening variables. *Psychol. Rev.*, 1948, **55**, 95–107.

McClelland, D. C., & Apicella, F. S. Reminiscence following experimentally induced failure. *J. exp. Psychol.*, 1947, **37**, 159–169.

Maier, N. R. F. *Frustration.* New York: McGraw-Hill, 1949.

Maier, N. R. F. Frustration theory: restatement and extension. *Psychol. Rev.*, 1956, **63**, 370–388.

Maier, N. R. F., & Ellen, P. Can the anxiety reduction theory explain abnormal fixation? *Psychol. Rev.*, 1951, **58**, 435–445.

Maier, N. R. F., & Ellen, P. The integrative value of concepts in frustration theory. *J. consult. Psychol.*, 1956, **23**, 195–206

Maier, N. R. F., & Feldman, R. S. Studies of abnormal behavior in the rat: XXII. Relationship between strength of fixation and duration of frustration. *J. comp. physiol. Psychol.*, 1948, **41**, 348–363.

Maier, N. R. F., & Klee, J. B. Studies of abnormal behavior in the rat: XII. The pattern of punishment and its relation to abnormal fixations. *J. exp. Psychol.*, 1943, **32**, 377–398.

Marquart, D. I. The pattern of punishment and its relation to abnormal fixation in adult human subjects. *J. gen. Psychol.*, 1948, **39**, 107–144.

Marx, M. H. The dimension of operational clarity. In Marx, M. H. (Ed.), *Theories in contemporary psychology*. New York: Macmillan, 1963. Pp. 187–202.

Marzocco, F. N. Frustration effect as a function of drive level, habit strength and distribution of trials during extinction. Unpublished doctoral dissertation, State Univ. Iowa, 1950.

Meyer, M. F. *The psychology of the other one*. Columbia, Mo.: Missouri Book Store, 1921.

Meyer, M. F. That whale among the fishes—the theory of emotions. *Psychol. Rev.*, 1933, **40**, 292–300.

Miller, N. E. The frustration-aggression hypothesis. *Psychol. Rev.*, 1941, **48**, 337–342.

Miller, N. E. Theory and experiment relating psychoanalytic displacement to stimulus-response generalization. *J. abnorm. soc. Psychol.*, 1948, **43**, 155–178.

Miller, N. E. Learnable drives and rewards. In S. S. Stevens (Ed.), *Handbook of experimental psychology*. New York: Wiley, 1951. Pp. 435–472.

Miler, N. E. Liberalization of basic S-R concepts: Extensions to conflict behavior, motivation and social learning. In S. Koch (Ed.) *Psychology: A study of a science*. Volume 2. New York: McGraw-Hill, 1959.

Miller, N. E., & Miles, W. R. Alcohol and removal of reward: an analytical study of rodent maze behavior. *J. comp. Psychol.*, 1936, **21**, 179–204.

Miller, N. E., & Stevenson, S. S. Agitated behavior of rats during experimental extinction and a curve of spontaneous recovery. *J. comp. Psychol.*, 1936, **21**, 205–231.

Mowrer, O. H. *Learning theory and behavior*. New York: Wiley, 1960.

Nissen, H. W. Description of learned responses in discrimination behavior. *Psychol. Rev.*, 1950, **57**, 121–131.

North, A. J., & Stimmel, D. T. Extinction of an instrumental response following a large number of reinforcements. *Psychol. Rep.*, 1960, **6**, 227–234.

Orlansky, H. Infant care and personality. *Psychol. Bull.*, 1949, **46**, 1–48.

Pavlik, W. B. The effects of deprivation schedule and reward magnitude on performance during acquisition and extinction. Paper read at East. Psychol. Ass., Philadelphia, April, 1961.

Penney, R. K. The effects of non-reinforcement on response strength as a function of number of previous reinforcements. *Canad. J. Psychol.*, 1960, **14**, 204–215.

Piaget, J. *The child's conception of the world.* New York: Harcourt, 1929.

Postman, L., & Bruner, J. S. Perception under stress. *Psychol. Rev.*, 1948, **55**, 314–323.

Reynolds, G. S. Behavioral contrast. *J. exp. anal. Behav.*, 1961, **4**, 57–71.

Reynolds, W. F., & Siegel, M. H. Drive reversal effect as a function of magnitude of reward. *Psychol. Rep.*, 1961, **8**, 135–141.

Reynolds, W. F., Richter, M. L., & Carlock, J. Resistance to extinction as a function of reward magnitude and number of training trials. Paper read at Psychonomic Soc., Chicago, 1960.

Rohrer, J. H. Factors influencing the occurrence of reminiscence: attempted formal rehearsal during the interpolated period. *J. exp. Psychol.*, 1949, **39**, 484–491.

Rosenthal, R. On the social psychology of the psychological experiment. *Amer. Scientist*, 1963, **51**, 268–283.

Rosenzweig, S. Preferences in the repetition of successful and unsuccessful activities as a function of age and personality. *J. genet. Psychol.*, 1933, **42**, 423–441.

Rosenzweig, S. Types of reaction to frustration: an heuristic classification. *J. abnorm. soc. Psychol.*, 1934, **29**, 298–300.

Rosenzweig, S. A test for types of reaction to frustration. *Amer. J. Ortho-psychiat.*, 1935, **4**, 395–403.

Rosenzweig, S. A general outline of frustration. *Charact. & Pers.* 1938, **7**, 151–160. (a)

Rosenzweig, S. The experimental study of regression. In H. A. Murray *et al.* (Eds.), *Explorations in Personality.* New York: Oxford, 1938. (b)

Rosenzweig, S. An experimental study of "repression" with special reference to need-persistive and ego-defensive reactions to frustration. *J. exp. Psychol.*, 1943, **32**, 64–74.

Rosenzweig, S. An outline of frustration theory. In J. McV. Hunt (Ed), *Personality and the behavior disorders.* New York: Ronald, 1944.

Rosenzweig, S. The picture-association method and its application in a study of reactions of frustration. *J. Pers.*, 1945, **14**, 3–23. (a)

Rosenzweig, S. Further comparative data on repetition-choice after success and failure, as related to frustration-tolerance. *J. genet. Psychol.,* 1945, **66,** 75–81. (b)

Rosenzweig, S. Revised norms for the adult form of the Rosenzweig P–F study. *J. Pers.,* 1950, **18,** 303–305.

Rosenzweig, S., & Mason, G. A. An experimental study of memory in relation to the theory of repression. *Brit. J. Psychol.,* 1934, **24,** 247–265.

Rotter, J. B. *Social learning and clinical psychology.* New York: Prentice-Hall, 1954.

Roussel, J. S. Frustration effect as a function of repeated non-reinforcements and as a function of the consistency of reinforcement prior to the introduction of non-reinforcement. Unpublished Master's thesis, Tulane Univ., 1952.

Schlosberg, H., & Pratt, C. H. The secondary reward value of inaccessible food for hungry and satiated rats. *J. comp. physiol. Psychol.,* 1956, **49,** 149–152.

Scott, E. D., & Wike, E. L. The effect of partially delayed reinforcement and trial distribution on the extinction of an instrumental response. *Amer. J. Psychol.,* 1956, **69,** 264–268.

Screven, C. G., & Cummings, L. The effect of nonreward and interference on variation in the amplitude of an instrumental response. *J. comp. physiol. Psychol.,* 1955, **48,** 299–304.

Screven, C. G., & Nunis, T. E. Response strength as a function of reduction in rate of subgoal reinforcement. *J. comp. physiol. Psychol.,* 1955, **47,** 323–325.

Sears, R. R. Experimental studies of projection: I. Attribution of traits. *J. soc. Psychol.,* 1936, **7,** 151–163.

Sears, R. R. Experimental studies of projection: II. Ideas of reference. *J. soc. Psychol.,* 1937, **8,** 389–400. (a)

Sears, R. R. Initiation of the repression sequence by experienced failure. *J. exp. Psychol.,* 1937, **20,** 570–580. (b)

Sears, R. R. Non-aggressive reactions to frustration. *Psychol. Rev.,* 1941, **48,** 343–346.

Sears, R. R. Survey of objective studies of psychoanalytic concepts. *Soc. Sci. Res. Coun. Bull.,* 1943, No. 51.

Sears, R R. Experimental analysis of psychoanalytic phenomena. In J. McV. Hunt (Ed.), *Personality and the behavior disorders.* New York: Ronald, 1944.

Sears, R. R. Relation of fantasy aggression to interpersonal aggression. *Child Develpm.,* 1950, **21,** 5–6.

Sears, R. R., Maccoby, E. E., & Levin, H. *Patterns of child rearing.* Evanston, Ill.: Row, Peterson, 1957.

Seward, J. P. Experimental evidence for the motivating function of reward. *Psychol. Bull.,* 1951, **58,** 130–149.

Seward, J. P., Pereboom, A. C., Butler, B., & Jones, R. B. The role of prefeeding in an apparent frustration effect. *J. exp. Psychol,* 1957, **54,** 445–450.

Shaffer, L. F. *The psychology of adjustment.* Boston: Houghton Mifflin, 1936.

Sheffield, V. F. Extinction as a function of partial reinforcement and distribution of practice. *J. exp. Psychol.,* 1949, **39,** 511–526.

Sheffield, V. F. Resistance to extinction as a function of the distribution of extinction trials. *J. exp. Psychol.,* 1950, **40,** 305–313.

Shoemaker, H. A. The relative efficiency of rewarded and non-rewarded training in a black-white discrimination problem. Unpublished doctoral dissertation, University Colorado, 1953.

Skinner, B. F. *The behavior of organisms.* New York: Appleton-Century-Crofts, 1938.

Skinner, B. F. Are theories of learning necessary? *Psychol. Rev.,* 1950, **57,** 193–216.

Skinner, B. F. *Verbal behavior.* New York: Appleton-Century-Crofts, 1957.

Skinner, B. F. Behaviorism at fifty. *Science,* 1963, **140,** 951–958.

Smoot, K. E., & Lawson, R. Performance after failure as a function of interpolated activity. *J. genet. Psychol.,* 1962, **100,** 205–213.

Solomon, R. L. The externalization of hunger and frustration drive. *J. comp. physiol. Psychol.,* 1956, **49,** 145–148.

Solomon, R. L., & Wynne, L. C. Traumatic avoidance learning: the principles of anxiety conservation and partial irreversibility. *Psychol. Rev.,* 1954, **61,** 353–385.

Solomon, R. L., Kamin, L. J., & Wynne, L. C. Traumatic avoidance learning: the outcome of several extinction procedures with dogs. *J. abnorm. soc. Psychol.,* 1953, **48,** 291–302.

Spence, K. W. The nature of discrimination learning in animals. *Psychol. Rev.,* 1936, **43,** 427–449.

Spence, K. W. Analysis of the formation of visual discrimination habits in the chimpanzee. *J. comp. Psychol.,* 1937, **23,** 77–100.

Spence, K. W. The nature of theory construction in contemporary psychology. *Psychol. Rev.,* 1944, **51,** 47–68.

Spence, K. W. The postulates and methods of "behaviorism." *Psychol. Rev.,* 1948, **55,** 67–78.

Spence, K. W. Theoretical interpretations of learning. In S. S. Stevens (Ed.), *Handbook of experimental psychology.* New York: Wiley, 1951. Pp. 690–729.

Spence, K. W. *Behavior theory and conditioning.* New Haven: Yale Univ. Press, 1956.

Spence, K. W. *Behavioral theory and learning.* Englewood Cliffs, N.J.: Prentice-Hall, 1960.

Staats, A. W. Studies on the concept of "abnormal" fixation. *J. gen. Psychol.*, 1959, **60**, 229–236.

Stanley, W. C. Extinction as a function of the spacing of extinction trials. *J. exp. Psychol.*, 1952, **43**, 249–260.

Theios, J. The partial reinforcement effect sustained through blocks of continuous reinforcement. *J. exp. Psychol.*, 1962, **64**, 1–6.

Tinklepaugh, O. L. An experimental study of representative factors in monkeys. *J. comp. Psychol.*, 1928, **8**, 197–236.

Tolman, E. C. *Purposive behavior in animals and men.* New York: Appleton-Century-Crofts, 1932.

Tolman, E. C. Operational behaviorism and current trends in psychology. *Proc. 25th Anniv. Celebration Inaug. Grad. Stud.* Los Angeles: University of Southern California, 1936, 89–103.

Tolman, E. C., Kurt Lewin: 1890–1947. *Psychol. Rev.*, 1948, **55**, 1–4.

Tolman, E. C. Discussion (from Interrelationships between perception and personality: a symposium). *J. Pers.*, 1949, **18**, 48–50.

Toynbee, A. J. A study of history (abridgment of volumes I–VI by D. C. Somervell). New York: Oxford, 1947.

Tyler, D. W., Marx, M. H., & Collier, G. Frustration stimuli in discrimination. *J. exp. Psychol.*, 1959, **58**, 295–301.

Wagner, A. R. The role of reinforcement and nonreinforcement in an "apparent frustration effect." *J. exp. Psychol.*, 1959, **57**, 130–136.

Wagner, A. R. Effects of amount and percentage of reinforcement and number of acquisition trials on conditioning and extinction. *J. exp. Psychol.*, 1961, **62**, 234–242. (a)

Wagner, A. R. The treatment of inhibition in the more complex behavioral situation. Paper read at Amer. Psychol. Ass., 1961. (b)

Waterhouse, I. K., & Child, I. L. Frustration and the quality of performance: III. An experimental study. *J. Pers.*, 1953, **21**, 298–311.

Weinstock, S. Resistance to extinction of a running response following partial reinforcement under widely spaced trials. *J. comp. physiol. Psychol.*, 1954, **47**, 318–322.

Wike, E. L., & McNamara, J. J. The effects of percentage of partially delayed reinforcement on the acquisition and extinction of an instrumental response. *J. comp. physiol. Psychol.*, 1957, **50**, 348–351.

Wilcoxon, H. C. "Abnormal fixation" and learning. *J. exp. Psychol.*, 1952, **44**, 324–333.

Williams, S. B., & Williams, E. W. Barrier-frustration and extinction in instrumental conditioning. *Amer. J. Psychol.*, 1943, **56**, 247–261.

Wilson, W., Weiss, E. J., & Amsel, A. Two tests of the Sheffield hypothesis concerning resistance to extinction, partial reinforcement, and distribution of practice. *J. exp. Psychol.*, 1955, **50**, 51–60.

Wolpe, J. Learning theory and "abnormal fixations." *Psychol. Rev.*, 1953, **60**, 111–116.

Wright, M. E. Constructiveness of play as affected by group organization and frustration. *Charact. & Pers.*, 1942, **11**, 40–49.

Yarrow, L. J. The effect of antecedent frustration on projective play. *Psychol. Monogr.*, 1948, **62**, No. 293.

Yates, A. J. *Frustration and conflict*. New York: Wiley, 1962.

Zeaman, D. Response latency as a function of the amount of reinforcement. *J. exp. Psychol.*, 1949, **39**, 466–483.

Zeaman, D. Skinner's theory of teaching machines. In Galanter, E. (Ed.), *Automatic teaching: the state of the art*. New York: Wiley, 1959.

Index